Studies in Graduate
& Professional Student
Development

Graduate Student Teaching Awards

Laura L. B. Border, Editor

Stillwater, Oklahoma
U.S.A.

NEW FORUMS PRESS, INC.

Published in the United States of America
by New Forums Press, Inc.1018 S. Lewis St.
Stillwater, OK 74074
www.newforums.com

Copyright © 2014 by New Forums Press, Inc.

All rights reserved. No part of this publication may be reproduced or transmitted in any form or by any means, electronic or mechanical, including photocopy, or any information storage or retrieval system, without permission in writing from the publisher.

Library of Congress Cataloging-in-Publication Data Pending

This book may be ordered in bulk quantities at discount from New Forums Press, Inc., P.O. Box 876, Stillwater, OK 74076 [Federal I.D. No. 73 1123239]. Printed in the United States of America.

ISSN: 1068-6096   Volume 15, 2014, ISBN: 1-58107-271-6

Contents

Introduction to Studies in Graduate and Professional Student Development xi
    Laura L. B. Border

Guest Editors' Introduction xiii
    Kathryn E. Linder & Stephanie V. Rohdieck

Section 1 — What Kinds of Award Programs Exist

Chapter 1 — Recognizing and Enhancing Future Faculty Teaching: An Inventory of Grants and Teaching Awards 1
    Justin E. Heinze, Laura N. Schram & Mary C. Wright

Section 2 — Creating an Award Program

Chapter 2 — Departmental-Level Teaching Awards as Part of a Mentorship Approach to Graduate Teacher Training 17
    Amy K. Marks, Kathryn E. Linder, Lauren A. Vermette, & Gary Fireman

Chapter 3 — Graduate Student Teaching Awards as Instruments of Educational Development 31
    Betsy Keating & Michael K. Potter

Section 3 — The Use of Portfolios in Awards

Chapter 4 — Using Teaching Portfolios in Graduate Teaching Award Nominations 45
    Stephanie V. Rohdieck, Kathryn E. Linder, Dawn Walts, Christina Holmes, & Kathleen M. Hallihan

Chapter 5 — Building Reflective Practitioners: The Benefit of Awarding Teaching Portfolio Development 65
    Allison Boye, Suzanne Tapp, & Micah Meixner Logan

Section 4 — Establishing Criteria for Portfolios in Awards

Chapter 6 — Using Collaborative Inquiry to Investigate Reflective Teaching Portfolios as Award Criteria 79
    Kim West, Leah Ferguson, Allison Henderson, Chantal Kawalilak, Colleen Krushelinski, Emily Morris, Catherine Neumann, & Serene Smyth

Chapter 7 — Identifying Excellent Teaching Through Graduate Student Teaching Award Nomination Portfolios 95
    Stephanie V. Rohdieck, Dawn Walts, Lindsay Bernhagen, & Kathleen M. Hallihan

(Continued next page.)

Section 5 — Foundations Needed for Awards to be Part of Professional Development for TAs

Chapter 8 — A Model of Professional Development for
    Graduate Student Teaching 115
    A. Ahmad & J. M. Barrington

Studies in Graduate & Professional Student Development

Editor
Laura L. B. Border
Director, Graduate Teacher Program
201 ATLAS, 362 UCB
University of Colorado Boulder
Boulder, CO 80309-0362
Laura.Border@colorado.edu

Associate Editor
Linda von Hoene
Director, GSI Teaching and Resource Center
301 Sproul Hall #5900
University of California, Berkeley
Berkeley, CA 94720-5900
vonhoene@berkeley.edu

Editorial Board 2006-2014

Elizabeth O'Conner Chandler
Director, Center for Teaching & Learning
University of Chicago

Alan Kalish
Director, University Center for the Advancement of Teaching
The Ohio State University

Tomas Lehker
Senior Assistant Director
Graduate Student Services
The Career Center
University of Michigan

Karron G. Lewis
Associate Director
Instructional Development Center for Teaching and Learning
The University of Texas at Austin

Heather Macdonald
Professor, Geology
College of William and Mary

Virginia Maurer
Associate Director
Derek Bok Center for Teaching
Harvard University

Matthew L. Ouellett
Associate Provost & Director, Office for Teaching & Learning
Wayne State University

William Rando
Director, Center for Teaching Excellence
University of Chicago

Dieter J. Schönwetter
Educational Resources and Faculty Development, Faculty of Dentistry
The University of Manitoba

Franklin Tuitt
Associate Professor
Morgridge College of Education
University of Denver

Review Board 2006-2014

Ann E. Austin
Erickson Professor
Higher, Adult and Lifelong Learning
Michigan State University

Falahan Ayorinde
Professor, Department of Chemistry
Howard University

Paul (PJ) Bennett
NANSLO Lab Manager
Colorado Community College System

Eileen Callahan
Director
Graduate Student Professional Development
University of Wisconsin - Madison

Henry Campa III
Professor, Fisheries and Wildlife
Assistant Dean, Graduate School
Michigan State University

(continued on page *vi*)

Christopher G. Carlson-Dakes
Assistant Director
DELTA Learning Community
University of Wisconsin - Madison

Tuesday L. Cooper
Walden University

Sandra L. Courter
Adjunct Assistant Professor
Engineering Professional Development
Wisconsin Center for Educational Research
University of Wisconsin - Madison

Daniel Denecke
Associate Vice President
Programs and Best Practices
Council Graduate Schools

Nanda Dimitrov
Associate Director, Teaching Support Centre
University of Western Ontario

Maureen Dunne
Memorial University of Newfoundland

Donna Ellis
Associate Director, TRACE
University of Waterloo

Chris M. Golde
Associate Vice Provost for Graduate Education
Stanford University

Jace Hargis
College Director
Higher Colleges of Technology
United Arab Emirates

Linda C. Hodges
Director, McGraw Center for Teaching & Learning
Princeton University

Trevor Holmes
Education Associate
Teaching Support Services
University of Guelph

Jeff Johnston
Assistant Director, Center for Teaching
Vanderbilt University

Kevin M. Johnston
Director, Teaching Assistant Program
University of Iowa

Katherine Dowell Kearns
Campus Instructional Consulting
Indiana University

Michele Marincovich
Associate Vice Provost of Undergraduate Education,
Director, Center for Teaching and Learning
Stanford University

Jeanette McDonald
Manager, Educational Development
Teaching Support Services
Wilfrid Laurier University

Kathryn M. Plank
Director, Center for Teaching and Learning
Otterbein University

Brian Rybarczyk
Director, Graduate Student Academic and Professional Development
University of North Carolina at Chapel Hill

Stephanie V. Rohdieck
Associate Director
University Center for the Advancement of Teaching
The Ohio State University

Kathleen Smith
University of Georgia

Rosalind Streichler
Director, Center for Teaching Development
University of California-San Diego

Lillian Tong
Faculty Associate
Center for Biology Education
University of Wisconsin-Madison

Mary C. Wright
Director, Assessment
and Associate Research Scientist
Center for Research, Learning & Teaching
University of Michigan

A peer-reviewed book series on the research, issues, and programs that address the education and development of graduate and professional students.

Publisher: Douglas Dollar
Circulation: Jean McKinney

Studies in Graduate and Professional Student Development is published once per year by New Forums Press, Inc., P.O. Box 876, Stillwater, Oklahoma 74076, to highlight those aspects of graduate education and the development of graduate and professional students to prepare them for the multiple roles they play on their campuses and for the professional roles they will fill upon leaving graduate school. The full range of issues involved in the development, programming, research projects, and administration of such programs is addressed by the series.

PRICES & STANDING ORDERS: Beginning with volume 11, this publication's content was broadened and the title was changed to *Studies in Graduate and Professional Student Development* (see page *ix* for details). Prices beginning with volume 11 are:

    List for existing single issues... U.S. $22.95
    Standing orders may be placed by emailing contact information to sales@newforums.com. You will be contacted prior to shipment.
    Overseas and Canada ....add U.S. $9.00 to above rates for each year.
    Call for information about bulk rates.

Please make payment with a check for U.S. funds drawn on a United States Bank in the Federal Reserve System, or with a U.S. Dollar World Money Order, or with a Postal Money Order imprinted in U.S. currency, or through your subscription agency. Send subscription requests to New Forums Press, Inc., P.O. Box 876, Stillwater, OK 74076 U.S.A.

SUBMISSIONS: See "Call for Papers," page *ix*.

ADVERTISING: Requests for classified and display advertising space rates and deadlines should be sent to the publisher.

COPYRIGHT © 2014 by New Forums Press, Inc. All Rights Reserved.

Call for Papers
Studies in Graduate and Professional Student Development
Laura L. B. Border, Editor
Linda von Hoene, Associate Editor

Studies in Graduate and Professional Student Development is a peer-reviewed book series designed to provide a platform for the discussion of the research, issues, and programs that address the professional development of graduate and professional students. Areas addressed include:

- Research on teaching, professional development, curricula, assessment and evaluation, training, certification, and career planning
- Research on effective disciplinary and interdisciplinary programs and workshop design, implementation and evaluation for teaching and learning
- Research on the transition from graduate school to full-time faculty positions
- Basic research on teaching and learning

The intended audience for this journal comprises:

- Disciplinary societies and their subcommittees on teaching and learning
- Personnel in the Office of the Graduate Dean
- Administrators, chairs, graduate faculty, and graduate directors
- Administrators, chairs, graduate faculty, and professional advisors in the professional schools
- Research faculty, research associates, and postdoctoral fellows at research institutions
- Faculty who teach departmental discipline-specific teaching methodology courses
- Faculty who serve as teaching assistant coordinators or supervisors
- TA development personnel at research institutions
- Preparing future faculty personnel at research institutions
- Graduate and professional student development personnel at research institutions

(Continued on page x.)

- Faculty development personnel at research, four-year, and two-year institutions
- Faculty who teach courses on postsecondary teaching and research on higher education in any department or in the School of Education
- Centers for Teaching and Learning
- Career development personnel who focus on nonacademic careers for master's and doctoral graduates
- Administrators and faculty at two-year and four-year institutions who hire candidates into faculty positions
- Graduate and professional students in all fields
- The Council of Graduate Schools
- The National Association of Graduate-Professional Students

To view authors' guidelines and subscription procedures, please visit the New Forums Press website at: http://www.newforums.com/

If you would like to submit your name to become a reviewer, please contact: Laura L. B. Border, Editor, at laura.border@colorado.edu

Introduction to Studies in Graduate and Professional Student Development

Studies in Graduate and Professional Student Development publishes articles on best practices, research, issues, programs, and assessment that affect the education and preparation of graduate students for their roles as teachers and scholars in postsecondary institutions in North America and beyond. The growth nationwide and internationally in programming to prepare graduate students not only as researchers but as instructors or teaching assistants for recitations and laboratories on the campuses of large research intensive institutions has been well funded by national agencies, foundations, and professional organizations (Austin, Connolly, Colbeck, 2008; Council of Graduate Schools, 2014; CIRTL, 2014; CGS, 2014). These future doctorates will become the faculty who will fill academic positions in approximately 4600 institutions in the USA alone, and more than 280 in Canada, and in the growing number of graduate level institutions around the world, including 50 that were created in the last 50 years (Carnegie Foundation, 2014; QS Top 50 Under 50, 2014, Government of Canada Publications, 2014).

Reflecting back on this gradual yet deep change in graduate education since the late 80's and into the 21st century, the commitment at the administrative, college, departmental, and faculty levels to change how future faculty are prepared is revealed in this volume, which addresses an award structure for teaching that parallels that of faculty. Professional development opportunities, such as training in college teaching, internships beyond the campus, and strategic support for writing, speaking, conducting research, and succeeding on the job market, are often the foci of academic reviews (Denecke, 2011). We are at a stage where fairly mature programs are being assessed, revised and up-dated, simplified and streamlined, focused and improved.

This edition, Volume 15, guest edited by Kathyryn E. Linder and Stephanie V. Rohdieck focuses on teaching awards for graduate student instructors. It addresses the recognition of graduate students as instructors and demonstrates the attention that university faculty members are devoting to the preparation of their masters and doctoral students in college pedagogy as well as in research. We hope that this preliminary work will stimulate even better practices and continued research in the field of graduate and professional student development.

References

Austin AE, Connolly M, Colbeck CL. 2008. Strategies for preparing integrated faculty: The Center for the Integration of Research, Teaching, and Learning. *New Directions for Teaching and Learning*. 2008(113):69-81.

Carnegie Foundation for the Advancement of Teaching. (2014). *The Carnegie Classification of Institutions of Higher Education*, downloaded October 2, 2014: http://classifications.carnegiefoundation.org/summary/enrollment_profile.php

Center for the Integraton of Research Teaching and Learning. (2014). Downloaded October 6, 2014: http://www.cirtl.net/About

Council of Graduate Schools. (2014).Preparing future faculty. Downloaded October 6, 2014: https://www.cgsnet.org/preparing-future-faculty

Denecke, D. D. (Ed). (2011). Assessment and Review of Graduate Programs. Council of Graduate Schools, Washington, D.C.

Government of Canada Publications. (2014). List of postsecondary institutions; downloaded October 2, 2014: http://publications.gc.ca/Collection/Statcan/81-582-X/institution.pdf, i.

QS Top Universities. (2014). QS university rankings: Top 50 under 50 2014, downloaded October 3, 2014: http://www.topuniversities.com/top-50-under-50/2014?utm_source=tu_house_banners&utm_medium=web_banner#sorting=rank+region=+country=+faculty=+stars=false+search=

Laura L. B. Border, Editor, 2014

Introduction to Graduate Student Teaching Awards

This volume of the *Studies in Graduate and Professional Student Development* series builds on a strong history of exploring the issues and challenges of graduate teaching assistant development that focus particularly on how we train graduate students and prepare them for their roles as future faculty. Past issues have defined the field, explored courses for teaching assistants, evaluated the effectiveness of certificate programs, examined the needs of students of color and international teaching assistants, and helped us to better understand how to prepare them for using technology in the classroom (2008). More recent volumes have focused on specific disciplinary preparation for teaching assistants (2009) and the context of how graduate students self-reflect on their identities as teachers and build community together through interdisciplinary teacher training (2010). The most recent volume, which mapped the range of graduate and professional student development programs, has further clarified the extent of programming and the need for further research and more in-depth understandings (2011).

In this volume, we turn to a relatively new development in graduate student professional development: the implementation of award programs to reward excellent teachers among our graduate student populations. For many graduate students, teaching is a central component of the training they receive during their course of study, but literature on graduate student teaching awards is sparse. In this volume, the articles cover a range of topics from what kinds of award programs exist, to best practices in creating your own award, to the tools needed to assess excellent teaching while also encouraging graduate student professional development. We are fortunate to have authors who can report on teaching assistant award programs across North America.

Graduate student awards for exemplary teaching are an important topic for us to explore. How excellent teaching is defined, measured, and rewarded has varied across institutions. Recent literature has attempted to help institutions develop reward systems that connect good teaching to student learning (Chism, 2006) and that encourage good teaching to be recognized at the same level as strong scholarship and research (Centra, 1993). As is evident from the articles in this volume, developing a culture of teaching excellence and a community of support for student learning has also become an integral component of award structures. As award systems for exemplary teaching become more institutionalized, this volume offers an excellent overview of the benefits and challenges of such programs for graduate students who are in the process of honing their skills to be successful academic teachers and researchers.

Section I: What Kinds of Award Programs Exist

As teaching award programs for graduate students continue to grow and develop, this volume of the *Studies in Graduate and Professional Student Development* series offers an opportunity to explore the range of programs that are now available in institutions of higher education. In Chapter 1: "Recognizing and Enhancing Future Faculty Teaching: An Inventory of Grants and Teaching Awards," Justin E. Heinze, Laura N. Schram and Mary C. Wright share their research on 21 doctoral granting institutions and their uses of graduate student teaching awards and grant programs for teaching improvement. The authors first raise the question of how motivational awards and grants are used for graduate student teaching improvement. The authors then share their findings on how extensive graduate student teaching awards and grants for teaching improvement are throughout the United States, and analyze the fact that awards are twice as common as grants despite the merits of grants for teaching improvement. Through an examination of the eligibility requirements and criteria used for each award and grant, the authors are able to identify three categories of awards that are generally used.

Section II: Creating an Award Program

In section two of this volume, we shift from exploring already existing teaching award programs to articulating the steps needed to create an award program at the department and institutional levels. In Chapter 2: "Departmental-Level Teaching Awards as Part of a Mentorship Approach to Graduate Teacher Training," Amy K. Marks, Kathryn E. Linder, Lauren A. Vermette, and Gary Fireman analyze the process and rationale for creating a graduate student award in a department of Psychology. As part of a paradigm shift from a teaching "assistant" model to a teaching "apprentice" model, the authors describe moving from a three-year model based on department teaching needs where faculty act as *supervisors* to a two-year training model that focuses more on graduate student apprenticeship goals with faculty as *mentors*. The development of a graduate student teaching award program as part of this paradigm shift calls attention to the ways in which graduate student teaching rewards can support particular cultural attitudes about teaching at the department level. The authors also offer recommendations based on their experience for best practices in the award development and implementation process.

In Chapter 3: "Graduate Student Teaching Awards as Instruments of Educational Development," Betsy Keating and Michael K. Potter also share their perspectives on how the development of a graduate student teaching award can be a catalyst for cultural change, but at the institutional-level. The authors present a thoughtful analysis of how teaching awards for graduate students can recognize a range of contributions to the institution. Specifically, the authors describe two teaching awards created at their institution: one for excellence in educational practice and the second in educational leadership. The authors find that the awards at their institution contributed to both consciousness-raising efforts about the importance of teaching and learning as well as to inspiring graduate students to be better teachers.

Section III: The Use of Portfolios in Awards

In this section, we look specifically at the use of portfolios for teaching award applications. By exploring the kinds of artifacts graduate stusdent teachers are asked to include in award applications that are structured as portfolios, we can learn more about the benefits and utility of teaching award applications for graduate students about to enter the job market.

In Chapter 4: "Using Teaching Portfolios in Graduate Teaching Award Nominations," Stephanie V. Rohdieck, Kathryn E. Linder, Dawn Walts, Christina Holmes, and Kathleen M. Hallihan share emergent themes from data collected in a study of teaching portfolio use at The Ohio State University. In addition to arguing for the representativeness of portfolios as an award application model, the authors also present evidence that portfolios can be simultaneously evaluative and reflective. Throughout their study, the authors share graduate student reflections on the utility of portfolios beyond the award application process, illustrating that portfolios created for teaching awards contribute more broadly to both professional development and job market preparation.

In Chapter 5: "Building Reflective Practitioners: The Benefit of Awarding Teaching Portfolio Development," Allison Boye, Suzanne Tapp, and Micah Meixner Logan explore how teaching awards for graduate students in a fellowship program at Texas Tech University serve a larger purpose in helping future faculty members enter the professoriate with confidence in their teaching. Through interviews with past award recipients, the authors analyze the benefits of creating teaching portfolios as well as the benefits of being recognized as a teaching portfolio award winner. Increased confidence was apparent in all of the interviews conducted.

Section IV: Establishing Criteria for Portfolios in Awards

Many of the articles in this volume state the importance of evidence-based decision making when choosing teaching award winners. Building on the previous section, Chapters 6 and 7 focus specifically on processes for establishing criteria for portfolios in graduate students teaching awards. In Chapter 6: "Using Collaborative Inquiry to Investigate Reflective Teaching Portfolios as Award Criteria," Kim West, Leah Ferguson, Allison Henderson, Chantal Kawalilak, Colleen Krushelinski, Emily Morris, Catherine Neumann, and Serene Smyth, share their experiences developing and using reflective teaching portfolios as the criteria for a graduate student teacher award at the University of Saskatchewan. The article, which was written through the process of collaborative inquiry, offers a fresh perspective on awards from the graduate student perspective. Based on their shared discussion, the authors are able to provide recommendations for award criteria and process.

In Chapter 7: "Identifying Excellent Teaching Through Graduate Student Teaching Award Nomination Portfolios," Stephanie V. Rohdieck, Dawn Walts, Lindsay Bernhagen, and Kathleen M. Hallihan offer an insider's view into how one university's graduate teaching award selection committee evaluated nominees' portfolios. By focusing specifically on the criteria used when scoring the portfolios, the authors note that evaluators found many forms of excellent teaching that were not on their original rubric. Based on this experience, the authors discuss the challenges and benefits they perceived in using teaching portfolios as evidence of teaching quality.

Section V: Foundations Needed for Awards to be Part of Professional Development for Graduate Student Teachers

In the final section of this volume, we expand our discussion of teaching awards from the institutional to the national level. In Chapter 8: "A Model of Professional Development for Graduate Student Teaching," A. Ahmad and J. M. Barrington explore the kinds of professional development needed to establish a strong foundation for excellent teachers who can compete for national award programs later in their professional careers. The authors outline a model for professional development that is based on a World Café style orientation, online components, and a graduate seminar, among other supportive programming. Through their article Ahmad and Barrington argue that strong reward programs also must provide strong professional development foundations.

This focus on the long-term success of graduate students is a theme that runs through many of the articles in this volume. By focusing on how to reward students for excellent teaching while also preparing them to excel in their careers, the authors in this volume prioritize reflection, intentionality, and clear criteria for success.

References

Centra, J.A. (1993). *Reflective faculty evaluation: Enhancing teaching and determining faculty effectiveness*. San Francisco: Jossey-Bass.

Chism, N. (2006). Teaching awards: What do they award? *The Journal of Higher Education 77*(4), 589-617.

Kathryn E. Linder & Stephanie V. Rohdieck, Guest Editors

Copyright © 2014, New Forums Press, Inc., P.O. Box 876, Stillwater, OK 74076. All Rights Reserved.

Chapter 1
Recognizing and Enhancing Future Faculty Teaching: An Inventory of Grants and Teaching Awards

Justin E. Heinze, Laura N. Schram & Mary C. Wright

This study examines the use of grants and teaching awards to improve graduate student and postdoctoral scholar teaching. Broadly, we differentiate between teaching grants, which are prospective in their scope, and teaching awards, which are retrospective and serve to recognize previous accomplishments. This study uses a sample (N = 21) of doctoral granting institutions in the United States and compares the frequency of awards versus grants, documenting the eligibility and criteria associated with each. We then present a further analysis of teaching awards and identify three common types of awards in our sample before closing with recommendations for the use of both awards and grants to improve the culture of teaching on campus.

Scholarship on teaching and learning suggests that newly minted PhDs joining the professoriate often feel ill-prepared to function effectively in their new roles as teachers (Golde, 2006). With teaching increasingly recognized as an important form of scholarship (Babin, Shaffer, & Tomas, 2002; Glassick, Huber, & Maeroff, 1997), programs and centers designed to improve or recognize quality of instruction are appearing in an increasing number of institutions (Kuhlenschmidt, 2011). How different programs work to improve quality of instruction is an important consideration for academic administrators. Graduate program and postdoctorial initiatives that emphasize the importance of instruction and thus serve to cultivate young teachers – in addition to young scholars – should therefore be of particular import.

Graduate student teaching grants and awards represent two such initiatives, both of which focus on the improvement of teaching in higher education. While both may motivate graduate students to excel in the classroom, more research examining the effectiveness of each approach in improving undergraduate instruction is needed (McAlpine & Gandell, 2003a). This study uses a sample of doctoral granting institutions and compares the frequency of awards versus grants, documenting the eligibility and criteria associated with each. We then present a further analysis of teaching awards, identify three common types of teaching awards in our sample, and discuss whether each type is likely to promote improved graduate student teaching. Finally, we close with recommendations for the use of both awards and grants to enhance the culture of teaching on campus.

Instructional Grants and Awards

Academic course development grants vary greatly in both size and scope. Typically, at the faculty level, teaching grants come in the form of summer salary or release time, materials and equipment to be used with the course, or access to certain facilities (Sunal, et al., 2010). In this article, we consider a *teaching grant* to be future-oriented in that recipients are expected to use the resources provided by the grant to improve the quality of their instruction through some future adaptation or intervention. Here, we use the umbrella term "grant" to refer to initiatives of various titles (i.e., grant, award, fellowship) used for future teaching improvements.

Grants are an important component of faculty work and typically offer value beyond just the stipend. For example, Neumann (2010) reported that national teaching grants assist in raising the status of teaching, an externality beyond the intended purpose of the programs. Similarly, at an institutional level, the presence of grants signals the importance of projects and legitimizes time and effort (Wright, Cook, & Brady, 2000). Teaching grants, then, can reflect an institution's commitment to teaching while also providing faculty with a justification for the additional time and effort that strong teaching typically requires (Bland, Center, Finstad, Risbey, & Staples, 2006).

Previous research demonstrates that grants encourage faculty to prioritize teaching and lead to innovative changes in the classroom (Eble & McKeachie, 1985; Marker, 1980; Pearson, 1998; Wright, et al., 2000). For example, an analysis of teaching innovation grant proposals over six years revealed that winning professors were able to introduce technological innovations into their classrooms that supported higher order and active learning (McAlpine & Gandell, 2003b). Moreover, many of the practices created under the grants later served as models for other faculty. Such studies suggest that future-oriented incentives can lead to improved teaching.

Teaching awards offer another opportunity to motivate faculty to be attentive to and improve their teaching (Feldman & Paulsen, 1999). In contrast to teaching grants, we categorize *teaching awards* as those that are received retrospectively and are in recognition of past excellence or other criteria. Just as the presence of grants can signal an institutional commitment to teaching, financial awards for exemplary teaching can convey the value an institution places on success in the classroom (Sorcinelli & Gross-Davis, 1996).

However, unlike grants, retrospective awards may do little to improve the culture of teaching on campus. Jacobsen (1989) found that a faculty incentive program based on past performance (student ratings) and need had no impact on teaching effectiveness. Rather, research suggests that, similar to grants, effective awards should be future oriented to promote further excellence rather than honor past achievements (Menges, 1996).

There is little work addressing whether and how teaching awards and grants impact graduate students or postdoctoral scholars. Despite arguments that future-oriented grants may be more effective motivators for faculty, preliminary evidence suggests that, for graduate student instructors, retrospective awards are more readily available. For example, in a study of teaching assistant manuals, Lowman and Mathie (1993) found that 17% of the manuals studied contained teaching award criteria, although none mentioned teaching grants. This suggests that teaching grants were either unavailable to graduate students or that they were not highlighted as an important aspect of their assistantship.

Despite the prevalence of both teaching awards and grants for faculty, more research is needed to understand how similar incentives impact graduate students and postdoctoral scholars' teaching. We take a necessary first step by updating prior inventories of graduate student teaching grants and awards (Lowman & Mathie, 1993). Although previous literature points to the effectiveness of future-oriented teaching grants as motivators for instructional improvement, we provide an analysis of criteria present in some teaching awards that have potential to develop graduate students and postdoctoral scholars as instructors.

Methodology

To investigate the extensiveness of instructional awards and grants for graduate students and postdoctoral scholars, in December 2011, we conducted a search at the websites of CIC ("Big 10") and Ivy League institutions (see Appendix A). We chose to sample these institutions because of their extensive graduate degree programs; eighteen of the twenty-one schools were among the top 50 doctorate-granting institutions in 2009 (National Science Foundation, 2009). Using terms such as "teaching award" or "instructional grant," we searched for all programs at an institution for which a graduate student or postdoctoral scholar would be eligible, even if in a team with faculty. (In other words, for the case of grants, even if a faculty member was required to serve as the primary investigator but the grant team could officially include graduate student/postdoc collaborators, we included this as an initiative for which future faculty were eligible.)

We focused on institution or school/college-wide awards, with the anticipation that these cross-disciplinary programs would have the broadest reach and impact on future faculty. We define "teaching awards" as initiatives that recognized a student or postdoc's retrospective achievements, i.e., instructional performance in past terms or years. In contrast, "teaching grants," were characterized by programs that primarily supported development of prospective activities, such as future course development or instructional innovations. After completing our search, we contacted institutions with only brief web descriptions of their programs to ensure we accurately represented the availability of each at each institution. With the descriptions, we coded both grants and awards into program type (e.g., grant for instructional technology or grant for assessment), and for awards, we also tabulated eligibility requirements and criteria.

Our collection method has several limitations; most notably, the institutions examined represent only a sample of colleges and universities that offer teaching grants or awards for graduate students. Additionally, our (largely) web-based search may have inadvertently excluded grants or awards that are not posted on university websites. Another by-product of our sampling procedure was the exclusion of departmental awards and grants, which omits a number of initiatives that are embedded within smaller units, such as teaching awards given to graduate students within one discipline. We also do not focus on inter- or extra-university initiatives, such as government or foundation grants as well as awards and support given by disciplinary associations.

Extent of Teaching Awards and Grants

Overall, we found that the vast majority (95%) of CIC and Ivy League universities offer graduate student or postdoctoral scholar teaching awards, at an institution- or college-wide level (Table 1). Only one school, the University of Minnesota, did not offer either school-wide teaching awards or grant awards. In contrast, less than half (48%) of these institutions offer graduate students or postdoctoral scholars the opportunity to participate in a teaching grant initiative, even as part of a faculty-led team. This discrepancy is significant given research suggesting that teaching grants most effectively foster instructional improvement, as described above. Notable exceptions are listed below, with fewer opportunities for graduate students, compared to postdoctoral scholars.

Assessment or Scholarship of Teaching and Learning (SOTL)-focused grants include the University of Illinois's Provost's Initiative on Teaching Advancement (PITA) which awards $7,500 to "to design, implement, and assess instructional innovation that has a high probability of enhancing education at Illinois," in alignment with the campus strategic plan (http://provost.illinois.edu/committees/tab/pita.html). Any instructional staff member, or a team from an academic unit, may apply. Indiana University and the University of Michigan have similar project-based initiatives, with funding from $2,000 to $12,000, to develop team-based Scholarship of Teaching and Learning projects (http://citl.indiana.edu/grants/sotlGrants.php and http://www.crlt.umich.edu/grants-awards/isl). The University of Michigan's grant specifically invites graduate student and postdoctoral scholar collaborators, while Indiana University's program is open only to graduate students as members of a project team.

Instructional technology-focused grants, like the University of Wisconsin-Madison's Engage Adaption Award, give $2,000 to support development and evaluation of assignments that use digital media (http://engage.wisc.edu/dma/about_award/index.html). Similarly, Harvard's Presidential Instructional Technology Fellows Program recruits graduate fellows to develop digital course materials (http://pitf.harvard.edu).

Cohort-based models, such as Michigan State University's Future Academic Scholars in Teaching (FAST), create learning communities to support the development and implementation of an initiative. For FAST, students meet weekly to learn about teaching and assessment, and they are given $1,000 for

Table 1: Presence of Teaching Awards and Teaching Grants at CIC and Ivy League Universities

	Teaching Award	Teaching Grant
Brown University	X	
Columbia University	X	
Cornell University*	X	X
Dartmouth College	X	
Harvard University	X	X
Indiana University	X	X
Michigan State University	X	X
Northwestern University	X	X
The Ohio State University	X	X
The Pennsylvania State University	X	
Princeton University	X	
Purdue University	X	X
University of Chicago	X	
University of Illinois	X	X
University of Iowa	X	
University of Michigan	X	X
University of Minnesota		
University of Nebraska	X	
University of Pennsylvania	X	
University of Wisconsin	X	X
Yale University	X	
TOTAL	20	10

*At Cornell, teaching center staff indicated that college-level grants and awards exist, but we were not able to verify their presence on university webpages.

project dissemination costs, such as travel to conferences. Similarly, participants in The Ohio State University's Graduate Teaching Fellows Program (located in the University Center for the Advancement of Teaching) complete a summer seminar on teaching and teaching support, and then meet monthly while they carry out a project "to provide ongoing, systematic teaching support to teaching assistants in their departments" throughout the academic year (http://ucat.osu.edu/ostep/gtf.html).

Grants with a more open focus include Purdue University's Teaching Academy Grants program, open to all graduate student members of its Teaching Academy, with grants of about $1,000 to support initiatives that impact student learning or an applicant's professional development (http://www.teachingacademy.purdue.edu/organizations/ceta.asp and Juan Velasquez, personal communication, January 18, 2012). Similarly, the Searle Center for Teaching Excellence, at Northwestern University, awards up to $1,200 for innovations that produce "new courses, new course materials, [or] new methods of assessment or evaluation" (http://www.northwestern.edu/searle/resources/innovative-teaching-grant.html). On a larger scale, the Harvard Initiative for Learning and Teaching's Hauser Fund gives awards of $5,000 to $50,000 for educational projects that are "innovative," "evidenced-based" and "extendable" (http://hilt.harvard.edu/pages/funding/). For both Northwestern and Harvard's programs, postdocs and graduate students are specifically included in the list of potential applicants.

In summary, relatively few opportunities exist for graduate students to engage in instructional grants, and there are even fewer prospects for postdoctoral scholars. Opportunities that do exist most frequently engage graduate students or postdocs in supportive cohort models, or as project team members, with a faculty member serving as the primary investigator or applicant.

Graduate Student Teaching Awards

As awards occurred more frequently in our sample than grants, we examine them in more depth in this section to determine whether certain award criteria have the potential to promote future development, in addition to recognizing previous success. To clarify in detail the criteria for the graduate student teaching awards in our sample, we contacted institutions with only brief web descriptions via e-mail and/or phone.

In terms of eligibility, there were two key screening criteria used across institutions: level of teaching experience and recency of teaching experience. Some institutions had no minimum requirements for level of experience, while others required two to three terms of teaching experience for graduate students to be eligible for an award. In some cases, as we discuss below, awards were restricted to either junior- or senior-level instructors. Regarding recency of teaching experience, some institutions required that graduate students teach at least one course in the last one to two academic years in order to be eligible for teaching awards, while others had no such requirements.

Award Emphases

We identified three approaches to instructional awards for graduate students and postdoctoral scholars: holistic awards, stage-based awards, and skill-based awards (see Table 2). *Holistic awards* acknowledge outstanding accomplishments by graduate student or postdoctoral scholar teachers, and they are by far the most common of the teaching awards (72% of the awards). The Ohio State Graduate Associate Teaching Award is another example that rewards:

> ... use of varied teaching techniques appropriate to course content and students; superior organizational skills in relation to course development and management; ability to stimulate thinking and develop understanding among students; excellent knowledge of and enthusiasm for course subject matter; resourcefulness in presenting course material; willingness to solicit and ability to reflect on feedback about teaching and implement changes for improvement; and ability to demonstrate that the course(s) resulted in significant student learning (http://www.gradsch.ohio-state.edu/graduate-associate-teaching-award.html).

Table 2. Graduate Student Teaching Award Criteria

	Course Materials	Teaching Effectiveness	Innovation	Development	Scholarship	Mentorship	Reflectiveness
HOLISTIC AWARDS*							
Brown: Excellence in Teaching Award	X	X				X	
Columbia: Presidential Teaching Award	X	X		X			
Dartmouth: Filene Graduate Teaching Award		X	X	X	X	X	X
Harvard: Kennedy School Dean's Award for Excellence in Student Teaching		X					
Indiana: Lieber Memorial Teaching Associate Award	X	X		X		X	X
Michigan State: Excellence-in-Teaching Citations	X	X	X	X	X		X
Northwestern: Weinberg College Outstanding Graduate Student Teacher Award	X	X					X
Ohio State: Graduate Associate Teaching Award	X	X		X			X
Pennsylvania State: Harold F. Martin Graduate Assistant Outstanding Teaching Award		X	X	X		X	X

Continued on next page.

Table 2 (continued).

	Course Materials	Teaching Effectiveness	Innovation	Development	Scholarship	Mentorship	Reflectiveness
Princeton: Friends of Davis International Center Excellence in Teaching Award		X		X			
Princeton: Association of Princeton Graduate Alumni Teaching Award		X					
Univ. of Chicago: Wayne C. Booth Graduate Student Prize for Excellence in Teaching		X					
Univ. of Illinois: Excellence in Undergraduate Teaching	X	X	X	X	X	X	
Univ. of Iowa: Outstanding Teaching Assistant Award		X		X		X	X
Univ. of Michigan: Outstanding Graduate Student Instructor Award		X	X	X	X	X	X
Univ. of Nebraska: Outstanding Graduate Teaching Assistant Award	X	X	X	X			X
Univ. of Pennsylvania: Penn Prize for Excellence in Teaching by Graduate Students		X					X
Yale: Prize Teaching Fellows		X			X		
STAGE-BASED AWARDS							
Purdue: Outstanding Graduate Teaching Assistants Award	X	X		X	X	X	X
Purdue: Committee for the Education of Teaching Assistants Teaching Award**		X					
Univ. of Wisconsin: UW-Madison Early Excellence in Teaching Award		X					
Univ. of Wisconsin: UW-Madison Capstone Ph.D. Teaching Award		X		X			X
SKILL-BASED AWARDS							
Purdue: Class of 1922 Helping Students Learn Award		X	X				
Univ. of Wisconsin: UW-Madison Innovation in Teaching Award		X	X				
Univ. of Chicago: Excellence in Course Design Award	X	X					X

*Other examples of holistic awards include Harvard University's Derek C. Bok Excellence in Graduate Student Teaching of Undergraduates. However, in this case, University webpages did not list significant detail about award criteria, and attempts to contact the university teaching center and/or graduate school were unsuccessful at eliciting more information to reliably fill in this table.
** Awards are made within departments, and criteria beyond excellence in teaching are determined by each department.

Stage-based awards acknowledge the accomplishments of graduate student or postdoc teachers at different developmental stages, and they more infrequently occur, comprising 16% of all awards. For example, the University of Wisconsin-Madison has an Early Excellence in Teaching Award for teaching assistants with less than four semesters of teaching experience, while the University of Wisconsin-Madison Capstone PhD Teaching Award rewards those who are at the end of their graduate careers. In this way, instructors at different stages of development are rewarded for their accomplishments. Similarly, Purdue University has the Committee for the Education of Teaching Assistants Award, which is a university-level award that acknowledges students selected by their departments for their commitment to undergraduate education. These awardees are then eligible for the Outstanding Graduate Teaching Assistants Award, which is the highest honor at Purdue for graduate students who have demonstrated excellence in teaching.

Skill-based teaching awards, only 12% of all recognitions, recognize graduate student instructors who have excelled in one specific teaching-related skill or ability. For example, the Purdue University Class of 1922 Helping Students Learn Award and the UW-Madison Innovation in Teaching Award reward graduate student teachers for development of innovative teaching techniques, while the Excellence in Course Design Award at University of Chicago acknowledges the accomplishments of graduate students in course design and student learning assessment.

Criteria for Teaching Awards

The selection criteria for evaluating evidence of excellence in graduate student teaching varied by institution, but seven categories emerged as the most common criteria for evaluating excellence in teaching (Table 2). Three metrics were utilized by over half of the awards: evidence of teaching effectiveness, evidence of development as a teacher, and reflectiveness on teaching.

All (100%) awards requested evidence of "teaching effectiveness," such as exceptional student work, significant impact on students' undergraduate education and/or future success, and evidence of student learning. Although this is most frequently assessed through self-reports (e.g., faculty and student letters), some institutions request exceptional student work or evidence of student learning. For example, the University of Chicago's Excellence in Course Design Award requires that candidates for the award include examples of student work and a clear articulation of assessment of student learning in the course. The second most frequently applied standards are "reflectiveness" (used by 52% of awards), most commonly assessed by a teaching philosophy or reflective statement, and "development" (also 52%), as evidenced by either peer assessments of teaching growth or participation in professional development activities related to teaching (e.g., attendance at conferences or conducting scholarship of teaching and learning).

Less utilized categories include "outstanding course materials" (40% of awards), "innovation" (32%), and "mentorship" (32%). For course materials, frequently requested documents include syllabi, assignments, and lectures, while innovation and mentorship were most commonly assessed through applicants' descriptions of creative approaches, as well as guidance of undergraduates and graduate students. Although not a frequently applied standard, in the case of innovation, a notable exception is the UW-Madison Innovation in Teaching Award, which "recognizes teaching assistants who brought exceptional creativity to their work and developed or adapted new teaching methods or techniques," as assessed through a faculty letter of recommendation and an applicant's personal statement (http://www.ls.wisc.edu/ta-awards/). No awards exist exclusively to reward "mentorship" in our sample, but several include mentorship of other instructors and students as a significant component of award, such as the University of Michigan's Outstanding Graduate Student Instructor award, which includes among the criteria "continuous growth as teachers (e.g., by seeking to refine their own teaching skills and helping others to do the same); and service as outstanding mentors and advisors to their students, colleagues and others in need of their help" (http://www.rackham.umich.edu/faculty_staff/awards/student_funding/outstanding_graduate_student_instructor_awards/).

Progress as scholars was the least frequently applied criterion, used in less than a quarter (24%) of awards. For the case of "scholarship," defined as progress to degree or research accomplishments, some institutions wish to prioritize the instructional aspects of a graduate student's role when awarding teaching, while for other institutions the expectation of successful scholarship may be implicit.

Discussion

Our inventory highlights a significant disparity in the number of universities that offer teaching grants compared to awards. Despite the merits of grants as potential motivators for innovative and effective teaching (Eble & McKeachie, 1985; Marker, 1980; Pearson 1998; Wright et al., 2000), teaching awards for Graduate Student Instructors or Teaching Assistants were twice as likely to be available than instructional grants. Further, of the grants that were available, most required the inclusion of a faculty member and/or project team. While not inherently negative for graduate instructors and postdoctoral scholars, such models may stifle autonomy or creativity for those instructors seeking to use grants for their course development. Although an intuitive recommendation would be to increase the number of grants available to graduate teachers, it is unclear why such a discrepancy in availability and eligibility exists. Future research may clarify obstacles to the expansion of grant programs for graduate student and postdoctoral teachers.

In addition to appearing with greater frequency, our analysis of teaching awards shows that their emphases tended to fall into three distinct domains: holistic excellence in teaching, specific skill development, and stage-based recognition. While each serves to recognize graduate students' accomplishments as instructors, we argue that stage-based awards have greater potential to impact subsequent classes taught by graduate student teachers and encourage development. By definition, stage-based awards require instructors to demonstrate an increasing level of competence with their teaching, which acknowledges that great teachers are made through increasing experience and dedication to their work. Further, criteria for later stage awards can be tailored to encourage instructors' independence and participation in mentorship or other career development activities. An alternate explanation for why innovation, mentorship and scholarship criteria appear with lesser frequency could be that they require a certain amount of proficiency and experience that is not expected of inexperienced instructors. Early stage awards, then, could focus on specific skill development, with more complex expectations (e.g., innovative course design; mentorship) for graduate students with increasing levels of teaching experience.

However, professional development activities should not be limited to more senior graduate student instructors. Previous research supports pairing professional development activities with teaching awards to better enable development as teachers (Sunal et al., 2010). While certain awards in our sample captured one or more of these aspects, their inclusion as criteria was fairly inconsistent. We suggest that professional development activities can encompass a range of options from more traditional (attending teaching conferences; publishing research on teaching) to more contemporary development activities (mentorship of other TAs; creating and maintain a teaching portfolio; teaching center certificate). Each activity offers more exposure to the teaching profession than would be possible through typical classroom interaction.

Recommendations

This study examines the availability and nature of graduate student teaching awards and teaching grants. Contrary to literature suggesting that instructional grants are a more effective way to achieve course innovation and positive teaching outcomes, the universities and colleges in our sample were far more likely to have teaching awards available. We offer several recommendations on teaching awards and grants based on the findings of our inventory. Most significantly, the merits of grants as potential motivators for effective teaching suggest the amplification of funding opportunities available to postdocs and graduate students to develop innovative initiatives. However, given the prominence of teaching awards, we also offer three suggestions about their structure.

First, design teaching awards in such a way as to resemble the future-oriented perspective of grants and thus motivate graduate student instructors to continually reflect on and improve their craft. A notable example that might be adapted elsewhere is Yale's Prize Teaching Fellows award. Student and faculty letters document past teaching effectiveness, but the award affords the applicant an opportunity to teach a class as instructor of record. In this manner, although the award recognized retrospective achievements, it also fosters future professional development opportunities.

Second, use stage-based awards which have greater potential to impact subsequent classes taught by graduate student teachers and encourage development. A noteworthy example is University of Wisconsin's two-stage model of teaching awards. While both the "Early Excellence in Teaching" and "Capstone PhD" teaching awards incorporate student evaluations and faculty endorsements, the latter also prompts graduate students to be reflective about their teaching and describe the evolution of their teaching philosophies. The combination of criteria (i.e., both external nominations and internal reflection) challenges more experienced instructors to think critically about the continued advancement of their teaching, all while maintaining a level of excellence in the classroom.

A final recommendation is to increase the use of awards that recognize the professional development of graduate student instructors and postdoctoral scholars, particularly their role as instructional innovators and their engagement in scholarship such as SOTL (the Scholarship of Teaching and Learning). Such acknowledgment signals the institution's commitment to the development of great teachers.

References

Babin, L. A., Shaffer, T. R., & Tomas, A. M. (2002). Teaching portfolios: Uses and development. *Journal of Marketing Education, 24,* 35-42.

Bland, C. J., Center, B. A., Finstad, D. A., Risbey, K. R., & Staples, J. (2006). The impact of appointment type on the productivity of commitment of full-time faculty in research and doctoral institutions. *The Journal of Higher Education, 77,* 89-123.

Eble, K. E., & McKeachie, W. J. (1985). Improving undergraduate education through faculty development: An analysis of effective programs and practices. San Francisco: Jossey-Bass.

Feldman, K. A., & Paulsen, M.B. (1999). Faculty motivation: The role of a supportive teaching culture. In M. Theall (Ed.), *Motivation from within: Approaches for encouraging faculty and students to excel: New Directions for Teaching and Learning* (pp. 71-78). San Francisco: Jossey-Bass.

Glassick, C. E., Huber, M. T., & Maeroff, G. I. (1997). *Scholarship assessed: Evaluation of the professoriate.* San Francisco: Jossey-Bass.

Golde, C. M. (2006). Preparing stewards of the discipline. In C. M. Golde & G. E. Walker (Eds.), *Envisioning the future of doctoral education: Preparing stewards of the discipline* (pp. 3–20). San Francisco: Jossey-Bass.

Jacobsen, R.H. (1989, March). *The impact of faculty incentive grants on teaching effectiveness.* Paper presentation at American Educational Research Association, San Francisco. (ERIC Document Reproduction Service No. ED305875.)

Kuhlenschmidt, S. (2011). Distribution and penetration of teaching-learning development units in higher education: Implications for strategic planning and research. In J. E. Miller & J. E. Groccia (Eds.), *To Improve the Academy* (pp. 274-287). San Francisco: Jossey-Bass.

Lowman, J., & Mathie, V. A. (1993). What should graduate teaching assistants know about teaching? *Teaching of Psychology, 20,* 84-88.

Marker, D. (1980). Improving the scholarly climate on campus through a program of small grants. In W. C. Nelsen & M. E. Siegel (Eds.), *Effective approaches to faculty development* (pp. 9-19). Washington, DC: Association of American Colleges.

McAlpine L., & Gandell, T. (2003a.) Teaching improvement grants: Their potential to promote a scholarly approach to teaching. *Journal of Further and Higher Education, 27,* 187-194.

McAlpine, L., & Gandell, T. (2003b). What they tell us about professors' instructional choices for the use of technology in higher education. *Journal of Further and Higher Education, 34,* 281-293.

Menges, R. J. (1996). Awards to individuals. In M. D. Svinicki & R. J. Menges (Eds.), *Honoring exemplary teaching: New Directions for Teaching and Learning* (pp. 3-9), San Francisco: Jossey-Bass.

National Science Foundation. (2009). Top 50 doctorate-granting institutions, ranked by number of doctorate recipients: 2009. http://www.nsf.gov/statistics/nsf11306/ (Accessed 1/31/12).

Neumann, R. (2010). Disciplinary differences and university teaching. *Studies in Higher Education, 26,* 135-146.

Pearson, M. (1998, April). *Issues in funding and supporting projects to improve the quality and encourage innovation in teaching in departments.* Paper presented at the International Consortium for Educational Development (ICED) Conference. Austin, TX. (ERIC Document Reproduction Service No. ED 423 737).

Sorcinelli, M. D., & Gross-Davis, B. (1996). Honoring exemplary teaching in research universities. In M. D. Svinicki & R. J. Menges (Eds.), *Honoring exemplary teaching: New Directions for Teaching and Learning* (pp. 71-76), San Francisco: Jossey-Bass.

Sunal, D. W., Hodges, J., Sunal, C. S., Whitaker, K. W., Freeman, L. M., Edwards, L., et al. (2010). Teaching science in higher education: Faculty professional development and barriers to change. *School Science and Mathematics, 101,* 246-257.

Wright, M., Cook, C. E., & Brady, E. (2000). *Using grants to enhance student learning.* CRLT Occasional Paper, No. 13. Ann Arbor, MI: University of Michigan Center for Research on Learning and Teaching.

Justin E. Heinze is a Research Investigator in the Department of Health Behavior and Health Education at the University of Michigan. He earned his PhD in education. His primary research interests include belonging motivation and developmental transitions in adolescence and emerging adulthood.

Laura N. Schram is Assistant Director at the University of Michigan's Center for Research on Learning and Teaching. She is responsible for coordinating several graduate student development programs and internationalization-related initiatives.

Mary C. Wright is Director of Assessment and an Associate Research Scientist at the University of Michigan's Center for Research on Learning and Teaching. In this capacity, she works with the University of Michigan's faculty and academic units on assessment of student learning, evaluation of educational initiatives, and the scholarship of teaching and learning (SoTL). She is also a member of the POD Network's Core Committee.

Appendix A
Graduate Student Teaching Award Websites

Institution	Award Name	Website
Brown University	Excellence in Teaching Award	http://www.brown.edu/gradschool/academics-research/brown-awards/excellence-in-teaching
Columbia University	Presidential Teaching Awards	http://www.columbia.edu/cu/vpaa/teach/
Cornell University	Cornelia Ye Outstanding Teaching Assistant Award	http://www.cte.cornell.edu/programs-services/grads-future-educators-tas/cornelia-ye-outstanding-teaching-assistant-award.html
Dartmouth College	Filene Graduate Teaching Award	http://graduate.dartmouth.edu/funding/teaching.html
Harvard University	Derek C. Bok Award for Excellence in Graduate Student Teaching of Undergraduates Kennedy School's Dean's Award for Excellence in Student Teaching	http://bokcenter.harvard.edu/derek-c-bok-award
Indiana University	Lieber Memorial Teaching Associate Award	http://teaching.iub.edu/awards_ai.php?nav=grants
Michigan State University	Excellence-in-Teaching Citations	http://www.ahr.msu.edu/all-university-awards
Northwestern University	Weinberg College Outstanding Graduate Student Teacher Award	http://www.weinberg.northwestern.edu/faculty/teaching-curriculum/teaching-awards/outstanding-graduate-student-teacher.html
Ohio State University	Graduate Associate Teaching Award	http://www.gradsch.ohio-state.edu/graduate-associate-teaching-award.html
Pennsylvania State University	Harold F. Martin Graduate Assistant Outstanding Teaching Award	http://www.la.psu.edu/awards/martin
Princeton University	Association of Princeton Graduate Alumni Teaching Awards AND for international grad student: Friends of Davis International Center	http://apga.reuniontechnologies.com/dynamic.asp?id=awardee_profiles_main Friends of Davis International Center: http://www.princeton.edu/~intlctr/friends/award.html
Purdue University	Outstanding Graduate Teaching Assistants Award Graduate School Excellence in Teaching Award Class of 1922 Helping Students Learn Award	http://www.purdue.edu/cie/teachingawards/awards.html

Continued on next page.

Appendix (continued).

University	Award	URL
University of Chicago	Excellence in Course Design Award Wayne C. Booth Graduate Student Prizes for Excellence in Teaching	http://teaching.uchicago.edu/?/graduate-instructors/excellence-in-course-design-award.html; http://chronicle.uchicago.edu/980305/awards.shtml
University of Illinois	Excellence in Undergraduate Teaching	http://provost.illinois.edu/programs/awards/campus/excellentundergrad.html
University of Iowa	Outstanding Teaching Assistant Award	http://www.grad.uiowa.edu/awards/outstanding-teaching-assistant-award
University of Michigan	Outstanding GSI award	http://www.rackham.umich.edu/faculty_staff/awards/student_funding/outstanding_graduate_student_instructor_awards/
University of Nebraska	Outstanding Graduate Teaching Assistant Award	http://graduate.unl.edu/awards/about/Guidelines_GTA_Award.pdf
University of Pennsylvania	Penn Prize for Excellence in Teaching by Graduate Students	https://provost.upenn.edu/education/teaching-at-penn/graduate-teaching-prize
University of Wisconsin	UW-Madison Early Excellence in Teaching Award UW-Madison Innovation in Teaching Award U-W-Madison Capstone PhD Teaching Award	http://www.ls.wisc.edu/ta-awards.html
Yale University	Prize Teaching Fellows	http://yalecollege.yale.edu/content/faculty-fellowships-and-prizes

Chapter 2
Departmental-Level Teaching Awards as Part of a Mentorship Approach to Graduate Teacher Training

Amy K. Marks, Kathryn E. Linder, Lauren A. Vermette, & Gary Fireman

In universities with limited doctoral-level training, departments may consider initiating their own graduate teaching training award programs. This paper presents information on how to establish such a program, and outlines a rationale for developing the award system while embracing an apprenticeship approach to doctoral-level teaching training.

Much of the literature on teaching awards and rewards in higher education focuses on the processes and structures for faculty rather than graduate students (see, for example, Bluteau & Krumins, 2008; Brawer, Steinart, St-Cyr, Watters, & Wood-Dauphinee, 2006; Carusetta, 2001; Knapper, 1997; Menges, 1996; Ruedrich, Cavey, Katz, & Grush, 1992). Notable exceptions such as Laurel Willingham-McLain and Deborah Pollack's article, "Exploring the Application of Best Practices to TA Awards: One University's Approach" (2006), typically discuss university-wide teaching awards for graduate students. At Suffolk University in Boston, MA, a private institution with a business school, law school, and college of arts and sciences that grants PhD degrees in only one field (psychology) there are too few graduate students for a university-wide teaching award. In 2011, the Psychology Department began to discuss the possibility of a department teaching award for the advanced graduate students teaching in undergraduate courses at the university. Of note, three of the authors of this study are affiliated with the Psychology Department and one author is affiliated with the university's Center for Teaching and Scholarly Excellence.

In this article, our goals are twofold: (1) to describe how to develop and implement department-level teaching awards for graduate students; and (2) to provide a clear rationale for why these awards are integral to creating a shift in the quality and satisfaction of graduate student teaching. Initially, we describe the university and department context. In particular, we discuss the rationale for developing the award and a paradigm shift that occurred within the department that necessitated a revision of the TA training program. Next, we describe the process involved in developing two department-level teaching awards for PhD students: one based on student nominations and the other on faculty nominations. From our experience with the initial review cycle of both TA awards, we recommend certain support structures for the development and implementation of department-level teaching awards. Through an exploration of the process and outcomes of the initial award cycles, we end the article with recommendations for those who are thinking of developing their own department-level teaching award.

University and Department Context: The Need for a Paradigm Shift

The Psychology department is part of a largely master's-level urban University located in Boston, MA, and has one of the most popular undergraduate majors, with 432 majors and minors combined. Our full-time faculty is comprised of 17 members and the department currently houses two master's-level graduate programs and a large PhD program in Clinical Psychology – the focus program for this paper. In recent years, the PhD training program (currently with over 70 enrolled students) earned a 7-year re-accreditation from the American Psychological Association. Like many competitive doctoral programs, faculty members in the department closely monitor current and alumni students' self-reported satisfaction with all domains of training. Students within the department have stated that they are typically "more than satisfied" with their research and clinical training.

One area of graduate training, however, that PhD students consistently rated as the least satisfying part of their doctoral training is their *teacher training* (e.g., a 3.5 satisfaction rating average, compared to averages in the 6's for other training areas; see Figure 1). In fact, recent surveys of graduate students in 2007-2009, revealed teacher training had evolved into their least favorite aspect of the PhD program. Many students noted that the variability in the teacher training experiences was vast, with comments such as "the TA experiences vary drastically by professor" and "experiences varied from semester to semester, and not all were great."

Perhaps not surprisingly, when faculty members were surveyed at the same time, they also provided low satisfaction ratings for the teacher training program, particularly with the quality of engagement from graduate students and support for their courses. Faculty gave an average rating of 3.2 (scale 1-5, 1 = low satisfaction, 5 = high satisfaction) for their overall satisfaction with the TA experience. Faculty wrote in comments such as "my TA was never able to come to classes regularly, so they were not really part of the course" and "it is clear that TAs are more interested in other parts of the program." Students felt under-supported by faculty, and faculty felt under-inspired by their students. It became clear a paradigmatic shift would be necessary to revitalize this cornerstone of the PhD training experience and bring it in line with the quality of the research and clinical training.

A Paradigm Shift in Teacher Training

Faculty endorsement to change our approach to teacher training was strong overall. Many faculty discussions in monthly faculty meetings centered on the need to revitalize doctoral student teacher training, and most faculty members were open to new suggestions from department administrators about how to proceed. The Psychology department aims to focus its efforts equally on undergraduate teaching and graduate training, and on providing quality instruction at all levels of the curriculum. With such teaching heritage and commitment, it was deemed by many faculty members as imperative to improve the teacher training experience and effectiveness for our graduate students. In 2011, the PhD program shifted our paradigm with respect to teacher training. Departmental administrators brought the question of improving teacher training before the full faculty at one of our earliest faculty meetings in September 2011. Data was presented to the faculty on both faculty and student low satisfaction ratings of the teacher training. The administrators invited discussion around ways to improve teacher training and offered a solution to change from the "assistant" model to an "apprentice" model. After this meeting, copies of the teacher training survey results and the training model descriptions were circulated to the faculty, and administrators invited further discussion by email. At the faculty

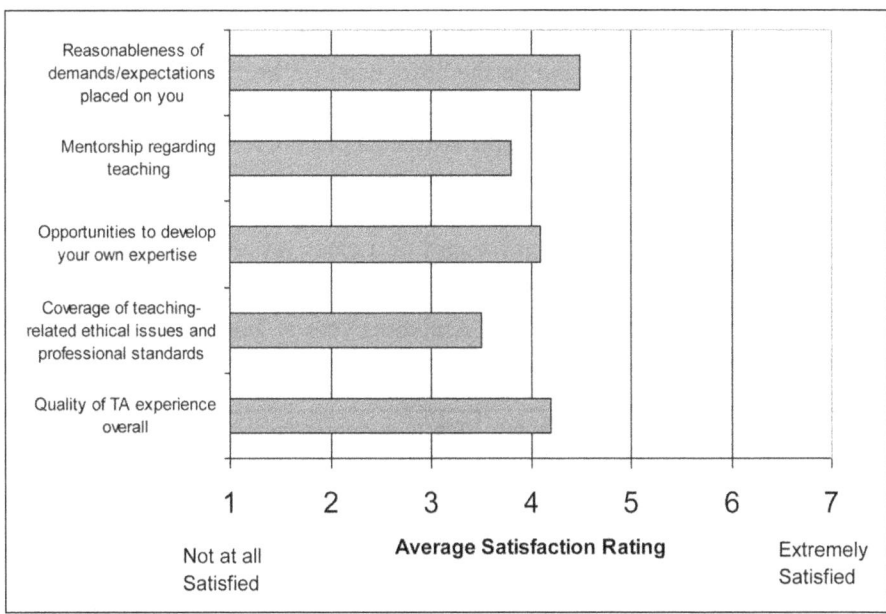

Figure 1. Graduate student annual survey 2010: Teaching Domain.

meeting in October 2011, administrators posed a motion and the faculty voted to adopt the new Apprenticeship approach, with minor revisions to the initial model description based on faculty email feedback.

What once was a mandatory three-year Teaching Assistant program became a mandatory two-year pedagogical Teaching Apprenticeship (TA) model. The former system relied heavily on administrative support tasks from the graduate student, such as grading support, photocopying, and holding office hours. Moreover, students were often assigned to courses based on professor needs and scheduling, with no input from students beyond schedule considerations. The new system implements a mentorship model centered on supporting graduate student TA training goals. In this system, students nominate both courses and professors with whom they would like to train, and based on their accompanying rationale and teaching goals, a match is made between student and professor volunteers. Table 1 provides a brief descriptive overview of the two teacher training systems, which were used by the faculty to vote in favor of the new Apprenticeship program.

Importantly, making a shift to the Apprenticeship model also required changes in faculty and student expectations about teacher training. Faculty were no longer guaranteed a TA, as in the old model, but rather were asked to volunteer to mentor a student each semester. Some faculty who had regularly been given TAs for many years made changes to their course designs to accommodate teaching without an assistant. Further, many faculty and students needed to shift their expectations of the TA experience from one in which the TA's role was solely to support faculty to one of a collaborative apprenticeship. There continue to be administrative challenges around this issue – on the one hand trying to provide faculty with the support they need to offer quality undergraduate instruction, and on the other hand optimizing graduate student teacher training. Faculty were also asked to meet more regularly with their TAs specifically to discuss the pedagogical aspects of course design and teaching, issues that might arise during the course, and provide direct feedback to TAs around their own teacher training goals. Faculty members were asked to provide a minimum of one class session (or part of a class session) for the TA to run

Table 1. Elements of the Teaching Assistant versus Teaching Apprenticeship Models

Teaching Assistant Model (old system)	Teaching Apprenticeship Model (new system)
Teaching assignments based on scheduling	Teaching assignments based on students' teacher training goals
Faculty supervise TA support duties	Faculty mentor TAs
Student's role in course is to support faculty	Student's role is to engage in all pedagogical aspects of the course
Considerable variability in faculty interest in teacher training	Only faculty interested in fully mentoring volunteer to take a TA

independently, with observation from the faculty member (many TAs run more than one class). On the students' end, we asked TAs to write out their rationale for selecting their course rankings, and to outline their own developmental teaching goals for the semester. The Director of Undergraduate and Graduate Studies has been responsible for managing the match between faculty mentors and TAs, fostering dialogue around TA training goals, and measuring/monitoring TA and faculty reviews at the end of each semester. At the year-end graduate student evaluation faculty meeting in May, we also devote considerable time drafting qualitative faculty feedback for students (which is delivered in the students' year-end evaluation letters) to applaud students for their individual teacher training achievements and offer areas for future growth in the coming year.

Development and Implementation of Teaching Apprenticeship Awards

With the an expressed desire from both faculty and students to adopt the Apprenticeship model, department administrators together next proposed the creation of two new doctoral student year-end awards which would focus on teacher training. The department already provided excellent support to advanced students looking for in-depth, mentored teacher training by offering a course in the Teaching of Psychology. Students taking this course often went on to teach their own undergraduate courses in the department. However, few rewards were in place to recognize students who were already thinking deeply about their teacher training in the early years of the program. With the new Apprenticeship model focused on graduate students' development as teachers, we now saw an opportunity to provide early and positive support to students showing early promise as educators. Whereas the department had in place many mechanisms to support early research training through student travel awards, small funds for master's level research expenses, and awards given to students for excellence in research publications and dissertation research, there existed no such incentives or accolades with respect to early teaching. The administrative members of the faculty saw an opportunity to place a higher value on teaching, on-par with research, by designing and offering two new departmental awards specifically for teacher training in the first two years of the program.

While the new apprenticeship model improved the value placed on teacher training, teaching awards seemed a convenient, low-cost, and attractive reward system to accompany our paradigmatic training shift. Because the literature on faculty awards for teaching has shown that these awards can "reward the 'wrong type' of teaching (e.g., reward socially popular instructors), or overlook the contributions of a large majority of conscientious teachers" (Wahlen, 2002, p. 45), it was important for the Psychology Department's TA teaching award to be one which reflected the merit and growth of the teaching skills the students were gaining (e.g., improved public speaking skills, creative active learning designs, and learning to accommodate individual differences in learning styles). While this award was meant to celebrate the most talented teachers in training, it was also emphasized as being part of a larger professionalization process for our graduate students.

With an eye toward creating new ways to integrate our undergraduate and doctoral-level programs, we decided one of the two awards would be an undergraduate student-nominated award and the other a faculty-nominated award. With only minimal back-and-forth among administrative faculty, we designed the following two awards:

Student-Nominated Outstanding TA Award. As part of the end-of-semester course evaluations, undergraduate students will be invited to write in a nomination for outstanding TA. Nominations will be made anonymously, should include the TA's name, and come with a description as to why the particular TA deserves the award. We ask undergraduates to consider the specific ways the TA went "above and beyond" in their role, and how the TA improved that student's learning experiences and outcomes. Departmental staff members then collect nominations at the end of fall and spring semesters from all undergraduate courses. All TAs (first- and second-year doctoral students) are eligible for this award.

Faculty-Nominated Excellence in Teaching Award. This is a year-end award is given to a second-year doctoral student who has shown a track-record of excellence throughout his or her time in the TA program, and who demonstrates exceptional promise as a future educator. Only second-year students are eligible, as the faculty have had four semesters to observe progress in teaching skill development across multiple courses and with multiple faculty mentors.

As is the case with all changes to departmental procedures, the faculty read, discussed, and voted to adopt the two new awards at a departmental faculty meeting. The chair of the department secured a modest amount of cash to accompany both awards (approximately $100, depending on funding), and departmental staff coordinated with the Graduate Student Association to add the award recipients to the year-end University graduate award ceremony and reception. The department chair and/or director of Graduate Studies attends the award ceremony and reception to present students with their awards in May. Student award recipients also receive public recognition by having their name engraved on a plaque displayed centrally in the department, and a congratulatory email announcement circulated to all department members.

Deciding on the Awardees: Process Considerations and Data

The main method of nominating graduate students for the department teaching award is through a ballot system where students and faculty provide their individual rationales for why they believe the graduate student instructor should win. This method is similar to the collection of letters of nomination from an administrator, faculty member, or current or former student, which Chism (2006) found to be the most common source of evidence provided for teaching awards (pp. 595-596). The department collected nominations for teaching awardees from students by offering ballots along with semester-end course evaluations in every psychology course. As part of the usual semester-end course evaluations, departmental staff circulates a packet of course evaluations for faculty to hand out to students in the last week of the course. Faculty and TAs are then asked to leave the room while students respond to the course evaluation survey, and a student volunteer returns the envelope with anonymous course evaluations to the departmental staff. A stack of student-nominated TA ballots (printed on colored paper with a description of the award) were included in the course evaluation pack, and faculty members were asked to instruct their students to fill out a ballot to nominate their course TA if they chose. The ballots contained a line to write in the TA's name, and a box to write in qualitative comments as to why they were nominating their TA. The three rating categories were based on the College's teaching evaluations for faculty instructor and course effectiveness. The specific instructions for the student-nominated ballot read:

> Dear student,
> The psychology department will be offering a Teaching Award to one outstanding TA at the end of the academic year. The recipient of the Student-Nominated Psychology TA award may have demonstrated excellence in one or more of the following areas:
> **Dedication to developing his or her own undergraduate teaching skills** (for example actively contributing to classes; lecturing)
> **Excellence in promoting undergraduate learning** (for example, going above-and-beyond when providing individualized assistance to students on assignments or during exam preparation; providing clear and comprehensive academic feedback to students orally and/or through grading)
> **Promoting a positive learning environment** (for example, supporting and nurturing student diversity in the classroom; understanding and working well with individual differences in learning styles)
> If you feel that your TA is worthy of consideration for this award, please nominate him or her by completing this form, and return it along with your course evaluations.

Wahlen (2002) has argued, "for good teaching to be properly assessed, it is necessary both to have procedures for assessing it, criteria for judging it, and documentation as evidence that criteria are met" (p. 81). In keeping with other practices used to determine departmental awards, the decision for awards is made with several considerations in mind. First, nominations must be made anonymously to protect faculty and undergraduate students from feeling coerced or deterred from taking risks. Second, the process for naming the awardees must be transparent. Chism (2006) has found that "levels of detail vary across the specified criteria" of faculty teaching awards (p. 594) and Menges (1996) found that "vagueness and secrecy foster suspicions about the objectivity and accuracy of the selection process" (p. 4). Carusetta (2001) agrees with Menges and adds that "the criteria used need to be open and explicit both for the nominees and the evaluators" (p. 38). Based on this literature and our own internal knowledge of best-practices with our colleagues, it was a priority for our department to make sure that the criteria for each award were clear to both the nominators and the nominees. Third, to promote another level of transparency in the process, all faculty members are given access to the nomination materials. All of the data are recorded from de-identified nominations and are kept in departmental electronic records which can be audited at any time by a faculty member. Further, faculty updates are made via emails and meeting announcements, summarizing nomination data and sharing the decision-making process fully. These considerations around maintaining anonymity for nominating faculty and students, and the transparency of the awarding process, have been essential to successfully establishing the TA award implementation process.

For each award cycle, departmental staff enters in the TA nomination and the qualitative comments from students into an Excel spreadsheet for data analysis. To determine an award winner, a two-step process is used to evaluate nomination data. First, raw numbers of ballots are obtained for each course, and the percentage of endorsements for each course is calculated reflecting the relative number of students in each class who nominated their TA. This is an important step, as some courses are larger than others, and can therefore yield a greater number of raw nominations.

In the spring and fall of 2011 we received over 400 ballots for consideration in the 2012 Student Nominated Outstanding TA Award for a total of 20 TAs. To hone-in on the most outstanding candidates for the award, we retained TAs for whom at least 50% of the class submitted a nomination. This left ten graduate student TAs in the running to receive the award, three of whom received more than 50% course nominations in both semesters. Those three were bumped to the top of the list for consideration, but the faculty continued with the qualitative comment analysis for all 10 candidates. Several considerations were used to rank candidates based on their qualitative nominating statements. First, many undergraduate students wrote in a TA nominee without qualitative comment. Six of the remaining ten TA Award candidates were eliminated from the running because of a very high proportion of missing qualitative nomination statements. This left four remaining TA Award candidates, three of whom had received nominations from more than 50% of their undergraduate students in their courses in both semesters. Upon examination of the remaining three candidates' nominating statements, there was one candidate whose nominating comments were clearly more detailed and superlative compared to the other two candidates. A sampling of representative comments made on behalf of the three final nominees is included in Table 2.

Examining the content of the nomination statements, the faculty unanimously identified a winner for the award. Though all three finalists received positive nominating statements from students, one nominee had superlative comments. The nominating statements for this student (nominee 2 in the table) were given with detail and offered a rationale that extended beyond the helpful, "good attitude" comments made for many other TAs. Nominee 2, the winner of the student-nominated award, made an impressive impact on undergraduate student learning, which was clear from the quality of nominating statements made by the students in the class.

Lowman (1994), in a study of the nomination letters for faculty teaching awards, broke down the characteristics most commonly associated with good teaching into five categories: intellectual excitement, interpersonal concern, effective motivation, commitment to teaching, and general positive descriptors (p. 139). Lowman found that "enthusiasm" was the most common descriptor used in the letters to describe why the student was nominating their teacher for an award. In award programs that name criteria of good teaching, Chism (2006) found enthusiasm, along with communication skills, organization, high standards, clear goals, strategies for student engagement, and a focus on higher-order thinking skills were the most common cited characteristics (p. 594). In keeping with these previous studies, we also observed comments about enthu-

Table 2. A sampling of representative nomination comments made for the three finalists for the student-nominated Outstanding TA Award

Nominee 1	Nominee 2	Nominee 3
[S]he is good Helpful, kind [Name] helped us stay on track Very helpful Always there	[S]he is the best TA I've ever had, always there to help, their emails were very helpful and simply being there for the students. [S]he is the best TA I've had at Suffolk, committed to the class and is always there to help!! Showed so much interest in everything we were taught; so patient when I had lots of questions. [S]he was incredibly enthusiastic about the class; always involved and I learned just as much from [Name] as I did from the professor. [S]he gave me great feedback on my paper and really made my writing better.	Gave good feedback Had a good attitude A great TA with a nice attitude Always available for questions, and has a good attitude

siasm and having a "good attitude" were the most common attributes used for nominations. A bit rarer were specific comments about the level of impact the TA had on the course as a whole, the TA's impact on the individual student's learning, or how the TA helped shape or cultivate the student's experience as a psychology major or student experience overall. The two winners we have had for the student-nominated award received comments that included enthusiasm-like descriptors, but also statements about how the TA affected the class as a whole, the student's individual learning and skills, or the student's overall experience in the semester.

For the faculty-nominated award, departmental staff created an online survey asking faculty members to nominate a student for the award if they had worked with a member of the second-year cohort they felt would be deserving of the award. Faculty members wrote in the student's name, and a nominating statement detailing why they had made the nomination. Staff compiled a final list of the nominees and statements, and set up a secure online, anonymous faculty voting website where faculty members could vote for one nominee. Both years we have given the award, two students were nominated by faculty. Each winner was selected based on who received the majority of the final faculty votes. All students nominated for the faculty award had demonstrated great excellence in their teaching abilities. In particular, nominees typically went "above-and-beyond" in their role, showing great dedication and enthusiasm throughout their entire teacher training experience, and a sincere, firm commitment to fostering undergraduate student learning. Faculty-nominated award winners spent considerable time scaffolding undergraduate student learning through creative study review techniques and running challenging and innovative laboratory exercises. The winners were highly organized and reliable, and in many ways were more like a colleague to their faculty mentor than a student.

Teacher Training and Award Outcome Data

Overall, our department has had a strong, positive reaction to both the paradigm shift to student-centered teacher training and our department-level award program. Additionally, in just the two years since our TA award system has been in place, we have seen (and measured through year-end surveys) improvements in graduate student attitudes toward teacher training. We have also observed an increased enrollment in the advanced Teaching of Psychology course (by about 20%). Average satisfaction ratings regarding teacher training have improved dramatically since 2007 and are now on par with other domains of our doctoral training program. Students are, on average, "mostly" to "extremely" satisfied with their teacher training overall, and 89% of students reported their faculty teaching mentors were supportive and responsive to their teacher training goals. In qualitative statements, graduate students described their appreciation for the shift in training model. One student wrote,

My teaching experiences so far have been great because I've really gotten a chance to get some hands-on experience on what it's like to teach and work in the classroom. While I did not have any formal previous experience with teaching, the professor with whom I was working was a great model and through her teaching, I was able to learn a lot of positive qualities that I hope to implement in my own teaching... I also really enjoyed being able to lecture for a whole class because it really opened my eyes to the beauty of teaching and I hope to be able to practice more during my training in the upcoming semesters.

In 2012, we sought feedback from faculty and students who have now been part of the new TA program for two years, and asked them to rate and comment on the paradigm shift and the awards program. We had a strong response rate, with over 85% of faculty and students responding. The data suggest strong support for both the paradigm shift and the awards. When asked how much they agreed with the statement "The department is doing a good job enacting an Apprenticeship model" all students responded with a rating of 5 (strongly agree) on a scale of 1-5 for this statement. On average, students strongly agreed (mean = 4.5 rating) with the statements "The teacher training program is a strength of our doctoral program" and "Overall, the mentorship I have received as a TA has been beneficial to my skill development as a teacher/educator." When asked to provide critical feedback or comments, most comments were very positive. Most positive comments centered on the benefits of mentored independent teaching opportunities in the classroom. For example, "My skills have improved under the Apprenticeship model as a result of guided feedback and inclusion within classroom activities." The critical comments (there were only two) focused on specific mentor-student moments or disagreements over teacher training elements (e.g., when or how to develop a lecture). When asked whether the TA awards acted as an incentive for their own development as teachers, our graduate students responded with only a mild agreement (average rating = 3.4), and provided comments such as, "They are great, but not necessarily the strongest motivation" and "intrinsic motivation is more important for teaching, but it is wonderful to be recognized." Faculty members strongly agreed (average rating = 4.5) with the statement "Do you think the TA awards have helped improve teacher training?" Comments such as "recognizing and rewarding good work is important" and "the awards highlight to TAs that the department takes TA training seriously and values TA performance" accompanied this question. Faculty members also were highly satisfied with the nomination procedure for selecting TA award recipients (average rating = 4.5), and with the validity of the overall process for selecting award recipients (average rating = 4.5). Interestingly, faculty responded only in mild agreement with the statement that the change in paradigm shift for teacher training has benefitted their own teaching experiences (average rating = 3.2). Comments for this question generally reflected the statement "I approached my TAs as apprentices before the switch, and so my day-to-day classroom experience is largely unaffected."

Recommendations

In sum, our Psychology Department needed to reconceptualize our teacher training program to better address the training needs of our graduate students. After a paradigm shift led to the development of a Teaching Apprenticeship program, we used two new teaching awards as tools to recognize students' efforts and growth as teachers under our new teaching model. The faculty administrators now typically spend approximately 15 hours of time per academic year reviewing nomination data and organizing the review process (e.g., via emails to colleagues and overseeing staff). The burden of the process rests more on departmental staff members, who organize the administrative aspects of balloting, create the online surveys, and enter ballot nominations into Excel. Through these various changes in teacher training philosophy and support, the Psychology Department was able to improve student satisfaction ratings regarding the teacher training program. The following key elements made this TA awards program development and implementation successful:

- The TA awards program was part of a larger movement to change the culture around teacher training. It was part of a paradigm shift to make a student-centered training experience, away from an administrative assistance-style teaching assistant model.
- Faculty members were readily supportive of the new awards, as part of a commitment to our larger University, which emphasizes the importance of quality teaching at the undergraduate level.
- Departmental staff members were already well-versed in creating online, anonymous voting systems, and department administrators were sensitive to keeping a transparent awarding process.

With these observations in mind, we offer the following recommendations to others considering developing their own departmental-level teaching awards:

Recommendation 1: Be specific about the criteria for awards and transparent about the award process. We learned from the literature and through our own mistakes in past experiences that trying to implement a training change in the department without transparency and specificity is quite useless. The overall process for re-establishing our TA training and awards was very smooth because we are committed to transparency and specificity. Transparency, for us, means making all documentation, data (i.e., ballots, spreadsheets), and award criteria readily available to all faculty members. Be specific in your questions of faculty and students when you are collecting nominations about the types of comments you would like to receive. This will increase the chance you receive meaningful ballots and data with which to select the awards recipients, and protect the validity of the award itself.

Recommendation 2: Protect the anonymity of nominators and voters. We paired the student-nominated ballots with the usual year-end-evaluation procedures whereby faculty and TAs are not in the room during balloting and are never in contact with the nomination ballots. For the faculty-nominated award, all voting is done online. This eliminates feelings of coercion or risk (usually experienced by junior faculty members) which were quite prominent when voting processes for other awards used to take place during faculty meetings several years ago.

Recommendation 3: Align your awards with your department's training goals. Developing the teaching awards would have made little sense in the department during the old assistantship model, where graduate student teachers were expected to provide primarily administrative course and faculty support. In that old paradigm with highly variable TA experiences from semester-to-semester, an uneven playing field on which to judge graduate student teaching skills would have threatened the validity of the award itself and of the awarding process. The teaching awards have proceeded smoothly so far in large part because they are aligned with explicitly written and faculty-adopted teacher training goals.

Finally, as we look ahead after just two cycles of the award, the department faculty would like to continue to develop our TA teaching awards process in the future. Our first step in this development will be to apply the criteria developed by Menges (1996) to test the effectiveness of our teaching award program itself. Once our program has gone through a few more cycles and generated enough data, we believe it would be beneficial to apply Menges's criteria to test the program and discuss any potential changes or revisions as a faculty. We also are planning a revision to the student-nominated ballot to include a statement encouraging concrete examples of TA effectiveness. Instructions are currently given verbally by instructors or staff when the evaluations are handed out, but it may be that not all classes are made aware of the importance of encouraging concrete examples of effectiveness in the nominating procedure.

References

Bluteau, P., & Krumins, M.A. (2008). Engaging academics in developing excellence: Releasing creativity through reward and recognition, *Journal of Further and Higher Education, 32*(4), 415–426.

Brawer, J., Steinart, Y., St-Cyr, J., Watters, K., & Wood-Dauphinee, S. (2006). The significance and impact of a faculty teaching award: Disparate perceptions of department chairs and award recipients, *Medical Teacher, 28*(7), 614–617.

Carusetta, E. (2001). Evaluating teaching through teaching awards. In C. Knapper & P. Cranton (Eds.), *New Directions in Teaching and Learning: No. 88. Fresh approaches to the evaluation of teaching* (pp. 31–40). San Francisco, CA: Jossey-Bass.

Knapper, C. (1997). Rewards for teaching. In P. Cranton (Ed.), *New Directions in Teaching and Learning: No. 72. Universal challenges in faculty work* (pp. 41-52). San Francisco, CA: Jossey-Bass.

Lowman, J. (1994). Professors as performers and motivators, *College Teaching, 42*(4), 137–141.

Menges, R. J. (1996). Awards to individuals. In M. D. Svinicki & R. J. Menges (Eds.), *New Directions in Teaching and Learning: No. 65. Honoring exemplary teaching* (pp. 3–9). San Francisco, CA: Jossey-Bass.

Ruedrich, S., Cavey, C., Katz, K., & Grush, L. (1992). Recognition of teaching excellence through the use of teaching awards: A faculty perspective, *Academic Psychiatry, 16*(1), 10–13.

Chism, N.V.N. (2005). Promoting a Sound Process for Teaching Awards Programs: Appropriate Work for Faculty Development Centers. In S. Chadwick-Blossey & D.R. Robertson (Eds.) *To Improve the Academy: Resources for Faculty, Instructional, and Organizational Development, Vol. 23.* (pp. 314–330). Bolton, MA: Anker.

Chism, N.V.N. (2006). Teaching awards: What do they award? *The Journal of Higher Education, 77*(4), 589–617.

Wahlen, S. (2002). Teaching skills and academic rewards, *Quality in Higher Education, 8*(1), 81–87.

Willingham-McLain, L., & Pollack, D. (2006). Exploring the application of best practices to TA awards: One university's approach. In S. Chadwick-Blossey & D.R. Robertson (Eds.), *To Improve the Academy: Resources for Faculty, Instructional, and Organizational Development, Vol. 24.* (pp. 247–258). Bolton, MA: Anker..

Amy Kerivan Marks, PhD, is an Associate Professor and Director of Undergraduate and Graduate Studies, Department of Psychology, at Suffolk University in Boston.

Kathryn E. Linder is the Director of the Center for Teaching and Scholarly Excellence at Suffolk University in Boston. Her current research interests include blended course design, scholarly writing productivity, and faculty development. Most recently, she is the author of *Rampage Violence Narratives: What Fictional Accounts of School Shootings Say about the Future of America's Youth* (Lexington Press, 2014).

Lauren A. Vermette is a staff assistant in the Department of Psychology at Suffolk University.

Gary Fireman, PhD, is a Professor and Chair of the Department of Psychology at Suffolk University.

Chapter 3
Graduate Student Teaching Awards as Instruments of Educational Development

Betsy Keating & Michael K. Potter

This paper explains the reasoning behind the development of teaching awards for graduate assistants and teaching assistants (GA/TAs) as part of a strategy of cultural change. Two awards were created: one for excellence in educational practice in the GA/TA role, and one for those who provide educational leadership beyond the requirements of their positions. Care was taken to develop awards encouraging, promoting, and honouring effective teaching and evidence-based decisions. Now that an award system—based on recommendations from the literature—has been developed and implemented, we have the opportunity to carry out research to determine its effects.

In 2008, the staff at the then two-year-old Centre for Teaching and Learning at the University of Windsor decided to create teaching awards for graduate teaching assistants (GAs) and undergraduate teaching assistants (TAs)—a task we approached with some trepidation. We worried that teaching awards were trivial and often meaningless, that they encouraged unnecessary and perhaps even harmful competition, that they reduced teaching to a popularity contest and a matter of performance, and that teaching awards would drain valuable time and energy away from more worthwhile projects (Chism, 2006).

Despite the concerns above, we wondered if we could create teaching awards that encouraged and facilitated meaningful educational development. We wanted to create teaching awards that called attention to not only the products and performances of excellent teaching, but the processes as well. If teaching awards could be used as instruments of educational development in its broadest sense, perhaps they could work as a force for cultural transformation.

That is the task we set for ourselves, and this is the story of what we created and why.

Educational Practice and Educational Leadership

We created two separate, but related awards: the *GA/TA Award for Educational Practice* and the *GA/TA Award for Educational Leadership*. Both awards are intended to publicly recognize and honour GAs and TAs who contributed to a positive, learning-centred university environment.

Each award recognizes a different kind of contribution—one through pedagogical practice amidst the fairly traditional confines of GA/TA roles, and one through efforts to improve learning experiences beyond such traditional roles. The former award sits more comfortably in the category of graduate student teaching awards as typically conceived. We wished to retain that kind of award on our campus, since GA/TAs are capable of excellence and positive contributions in such roles. Also, although many GAs and TAs will not have the time to pursue the more ambitious sorts of activities recognized by the second award, we wanted to encourage such activities as well, so we created an award that would encourage and honour contributions that positively affected the learning environment beyond the course level. To avoid category errors (the same award being given to individuals for activities that are so substantially dissimilar that there is no logic to their membership in the same category), we abandoned, early on, the notion of recognizing both kinds of educational excellence with one award.

Recognizing those who make such positive contributions is one thing, but we decided early in the process that we did not want the award to be a mere honour. Rather, it should be a means of inspiring those who previously thought such excellence was beyond their reach and those who may not have known that such achievements were a possibility for GAs and TAs. This consciousness-raising purpose would need to be reflected in our choice of criteria, so that the criteria as a set would provide potential applicants with a glimpse of the vast possibilities inherent in their roles.

Another aspect of consciousness-raising was also part of the cultural agenda behind the creation of these awards: to bring examples of educational excellence to the attention of everyone in our university community, thereby generating awareness about what is possible in higher education and developing a sense of pride in the teaching and learning opportunities available.

Our centre is located in a mid-sized Canadian university of approximately 16,000 students. The University of Windsor has a comprehensive array of faculties and programs including over 1,600 graduate students in 60 different programs. International students make up approximately 11 percent of the student population. At the time of this writing, the University employs 855 GAs and TAs. Our university does not have a long history of educational development—our centre, for instance, is barely five years old, and most of our programs are three years old at best—so our faculty members, sessional instructors, GA/TAs, and administrators tend to be quite traditional in their conception of what it means to teach well, wedded to the notion of teaching as an amateur occupation forced upon often reluctant researchers. They also tend to be suspicious of the very notion of scholarly teaching, or even that there can be such a thing as excellence in teaching beyond well-organized notes. Changing this culture is a large part of our mandate. Recognizing that nothing convinces as well as success, we intended to publicize successes that may shift current beliefs about teaching.

Aside from these commonalities in overall intent, each award has its own set of criteria, which were chosen for a balance of specificity and flexibility as well as for their contributions to the program's purposes. Although the criteria, nomination process, and evaluation process were determined primarily through reason, we were also influenced by the programs at the institutions we surveyed and by the suggestions for improved teaching award programs set out by Sorcinelli & Gross Davis (1996).

Background and Reasoning

We found relatively little published research on graduate student teaching awards from Canadian sources, so we began to investigate the types of graduate student teaching awards offered at Canadian universities. Information about these awards was gathered from university websites. We were cognizant that some of the information gathered by this means might be out-of-date or less than comprehensive; however, our purpose was to gather a general impression of the state of graduate student teaching awards offered by Canadian universities and to find out if there were outstanding models that merited further investigation.

Of the 27 Canadian universities identified as similar to the University of Windsor in size and purpose, 15 offered graduate student teaching awards. Common characteristics and patterns were simple to spot. In some universities, graduate student teaching awards were handled in a central location, in others they were scattered through individual departments, and in many there were combinations of both. Well-established teaching and learning centres with an extensive array of programs tended to have more formalized awards processes and more specific criteria. There also seemed to be a fairly recent drive in these universities to offer more centralized awards—many centralized award programs had been in existence for fewer than five years. Department, faculty, or discipline-based graduate student teaching awards appeared to have a longer history, though they also tended to be less formalized and more general in their requirements and criteria. They appeared to be less well defined in terms of specific criteria for teaching excellence as opposed to research, academic achievement, popularity, or other implied factors.

The content of the awards varied greatly. Some included cash prizes ranging from $200 - $1,000. Others included one or several of the following: names engraved on university-displayed plaques; books; certificates; commendations at award ceremonies and/or convocation; and public recognition on awards websites, newsletters, and/or press releases.

There was also variety in the number of awards offered in any given year. The majority of universities offer between one and three awards, but some ranged up to unlimited inclusivity of all nominees.

We found some confirmation of our general anxieties regarding awards as well. The nomination requirements for many awards consisted of just a letter from one or more nominators. In some cases, the nominator need not be anyone with detailed knowledge of, or experience with, the nominee's teaching. One award required the nominator to be someone familiar with the nominee's *research*, which indicates a conceptual confusion regarding the purpose of a teaching award. Most awards also required other letters of support, some specifying that these must be written by current or former students of the nominee. For most of the graduate student teaching awards we found, these were the only requirements: a nomination letter plus one or more letters of support.

Some of the graduate student teaching awards as described on the universities' websites did require more in the application package. Three awards specified that a summary of student evaluation scores be included, one required a curriculum vitae, one required a transcript, one required a teaching philosophy (without a dossier), and two required a teaching dossier (presumably including a teaching philosophy). In some cases what was *said* about the purpose of such awards was at odds with what was *required* in the applications. If, for instance, an award program is solely intended to shine a spotlight on examples of effective teaching, a curriculum vitae is irrelevant. If there are additional purposes for the award, some of those may make curriculum vitae relevant. On the other hand, it is more difficult to imagine what could make an academic transcript relevant to a teaching award.

In many cases criteria were indicated that did not seem to be criteria at all, but rather vague restatements of the award's purpose. Some programs stated criteria that every graduate student in a teaching role would meet by necessity to some extent (i.e. "contributes to student learning experience") rendering those criteria unproductive. Problems with criteria for teaching awards have been identified by others, notably Chism (2006), who speculated on the causes of this problem: "the primacy of the symbolic—rather than individual reward function—of many programs; the belief that excellent teaching is impossible to define because it is ineffable, situation-specific, or individual; the belief that everyone knows good teaching when he or she sees it; or the lack of knowledge of the research literature on teaching (or lack of trust of these findings) on the part of those who frame the awards" (p. 601).

Some programs did state clear criteria, often as personal characteristics that applicants should exhibit. As expected, there was considerable overlap in these criteria—terms like dedication/commitment, enthusiasm, organization, and inspiration were common. Other programs used skills as criteria—skills in communication, feedback, and clear presentation were common. A few used broader categories—such as "teaching skills"—instead.

We found a few graduate student teaching award programs that gave us hope. The programs that required teaching dossiers, for instance, appeared much more thoughtful in their design. The process of putting together a teaching dossier can, in itself, encourage worthwhile critical reflection and a consequently deeper understanding of one's practice (Carraccio & Englander, 2004; Knapper & Wilcox, 2007; Knapper & Wright, 2001) —aspects of scholarly teaching (Potter & Kustra, 2011) that should provide applicants with an opportunity for self-development.

From these findings we took the following lessons:

1. Require that the nominator has detailed knowledge of the nominee's teaching.
2. Include input from the nominee's students.
3. Require more evidence than letters of support. Without a doubt, letters of support have a legitimate role to play in such programs, but if awards are to be more than popularity contests, then they should also require evidence of learning and other effects, critical refection, and/or a scholarly basis for practice.
4. Make a teaching dossier one of the requirements. If the process of applying for a teaching award is intended to be developmental, it must encourage applicants to gather and reflect on evidence of the effects of their teaching, provide structural guidance to help applicants engage with that process fruitfully, and require evidence that is in some way relevant to effective and/or scholarly teaching.
5. Align our application requirements with the stated purpose of the awards.
6. Make the adjudication criteria clear and specific. Make sure the criteria reflect a diversity of pedagogical approaches and the conceptions of teaching our centre wishes to promote.

Between exploring the published material on successful teaching awards and locating some potential bits and pieces of exemplars in Canadian universities, we were left with the sense that it would be possible to create a graduate student teaching award program that suited our purposes. Although it might be unusual and difficult, we concluded it would be possible to create a program that encouraged and supported processes of educational development, influenced positive cultural changes regarding teaching, actually recognized effective and/or scholarly teaching practices, and set clear, high and achievable expectations.

Award Specifics

The GA/TA Award for Educational Practice honours a GA or TA (or team of GA/TAs) who has *enhanced, maximized, or deepened student learning* through at least four of the following means:

- Effectively using scholarly and/or learning-centred strategies, methods, techniques, and learning experiences.
- Effectively using scholarly and/or learning-centred assessment and feedback strategies, methods, techniques, or models.
- Incorporating practical, transferable skill development (communication, problem-solving, critical thinking, creative thinking, literacy, numeracy, teamwork, leadership, love of life-long learning) into learning experiences, consistent with the University of Windsor graduate attributes.
- Modeling high standards and expectations, reliability, availability, integrity, adaptability, respect, honesty, caring, and responsibility as a teacher.
- Interacting with students in such a way that they feel inspired, motivated, engaged, and critically challenged.
- Creating or contributing to a positive learning-centred environment for University of Windsor students.

These criteria are intended to communicate the message that the award is intended to honour teaching that is either demonstrably excellent or demonstrably likely to be excellent. Thus, the connection between teaching and student learning is made explicit from the outset. The criteria recognize a range of practices that may contribute to student learning, recognizing that teaching involves far more than mere lecturing. This is especially important at a traditionalist and conservative university. The criteria encourage nominees and nominators to see teaching as a potentially scholarly activity, and tie the notion of scholarly teaching to learning-centredness (not learner-centredness), which has become part of the University's vision. The University's graduate attributes are mentioned explicitly, and the criteria frame them in terms of skills that can be integrated into learning experiences, which typically focus on content acquisition. Modeling high standards is recognized as crucial, and the standards we wish to encourage are laid out explicitly. Finally, the kinds of professor-student interactions we wish to encourage are also made explicit as part of the criteria.

Thus, the award criteria not only describe the kind of teaching we are interested in awarding, but also frames what it means to be a good teacher in such a way that, we hope, any potential nominee or nominator reading them would be likely to come away with a slightly broadened perspective.

The second award seeks to empower and encourage a broader vision of educational change and commitment. The GA/TA Award for Educational Leadership honours a GA or TA (or team of GA/TAs) who has *played an active role in shaping or transforming the teaching and learning environment of the University of Windsor*, through at least three of the following means:

- Initiating, facilitating, or coordinating efforts to improve the teaching and learning environment at the departmental, faculty, or institutional levels. This may include:
    - Leading, individually or in collaboration with others, teaching and learning events at the departmental, faculty, or institutional level—such as open houses, GATAcademy, science fairs, teaching and learning conferences, workshops, seminars, discussion groups, and learning communities.
    - Organizing, creating or otherwise leading initiatives for pedagogical information-sharing, skill-development, or pedagogical innovation, among GA/TAs at the departmental, faculty, or institutional level—such as a GA/TA guide, wiki, website, journal, or newsletter.
- Promoting and helping others to implement scholarly and/or learning-centred strategies, methods, and techniques in instruction, assessment, mentorship, or other forms of teaching.
- Identifying and solving, by oneself or in collaboration with others, teaching and learning problems at the departmental, faculty, or institutional level.
- Participating as a student representative in curriculum refinement and development activities at the departmental, faculty, or institutional level.
- Effectively mentoring other GA/TAs in teaching and learning, while modeling high standards and expectations, reliability, availability, integrity, adaptability, respect, honesty, caring, and responsibility as a teacher.

These criteria build on and extend the criteria for the Educational Practice award. Again, the criteria are intended to both set out the necessary requirements for the award and encourage a certain vision of what educational leadership could and should look like. We intend to encourage GA/TAs to take an active role in transforming the educational cultures of their departments, faculties, and the institution. This active role can take many forms, as we try to recognize and highlight. We also want to move academics away from seeing leadership as something that one does individually (the "heroic" conception of leadership) by calling attention to collaborative and service-oriented leadership, mentoring, and involvement in committee work relevant to teaching and learning.

The Nomination and Evaluation Processes

The entire nomination and evaluation process is detailed publicly in order to make it clear that these awards are not popularity contests, nepotistic exercises, nor public relations exercises, as per our initial concerns about teaching awards and Sorcinelli and Gross Davis's (1996) first recommendation for improving such awards. This section draws extensively from the information provided to potential nominees and nominators on our centre's website (www.uwindsor.ca/ctl).

All nominees must submit a dossier, typically created with the nominator(s) and often in consultation with the chair of the GA/TA awards committee, who guides and facilitates the evaluation of dossiers, but does not vote. Nominees and nominators are strongly encouraged to contact and work with the committee chair. The nomination dossiers are strategically targeted teaching dossiers focused on demonstrating achievement of the criteria for GA/TA awards. Such dossiers may not necessarily communicate the quality of a nominee's teaching or educational leadership—it is at least possible for a good dossier to make a mediocre teacher look exemplary, though in our experience it is more common for a poor dossier to make an exemplary teacher look mediocre. Dossiers are representations only, containing the evidence we must rely upon to make decisions (Leverenz & Goodburn, 1998). One reason nominees are encouraged to work with the committee chair in preparing their dossiers is to ensure that the dossiers adequately represent their ability and achievements. Nominees may meet with the chair as many times as they wish, to ask questions, seek clarification, and receive feedback to improve their dossiers.

This requirement is unusual at our institution, so many faculty members and graduate students resisted it at first, decrying it as a lot of work for little gain. Some faculty members complained that they would not nominate their GA/TAs for the awards *because* the dossier required too much work. We responded to such complaints by acknowledging that the process requires commitment, time, and work—then explaining the purpose of the awards and the reasoning behind our process. Most other awards at our institution had no explicit criteria and required little more than an email from a nominee, while some required a summary of student evaluation of teaching (SET) scores. Given the developmental and cultural goals of our awards, we believe it necessary to maintain a commitment to the integrity of the nomination and evaluation process, and especially to the necessity of evidence, as collected and explained in the dossier. Despite such resistance, from the outset nominees and nominators who work through the process of creating their dossiers comment that it is worth the effort, even if they do not win. The process of creating a good nomination dossier is intended to inspire and guide reflection on what really mattered to nominees as teachers. We believe that by requiring nominees to provide evidence of the effects of their teaching, the notion of scholarly teaching may begin to crystallize in their minds. More practically, this process ensures that the award committee can base its decision as much as possible on evidence rather than conjecture.

We decided we would accept as many as three winners for each award per year, depending on the quality of nominations, which average eight per year for the Educational Practice award and three per year for Educational Leadership. Due to our commitment to protecting the integrity of the awards, we sometimes present fewer awards than the maximum—in 2009 we presented two awards for Educational Practice and one for Educational Leadership; in 2010, we presented three awards for Educational Practice and three for Educational Leadership; in 2011, we presented two awards for Educational Practice and one for Educational Leadership; and in 2012, when the number of nominations doubled, we presented three awards for Educational Practice and three for Educational Leadership.

There are four steps to the nomination process. First, nominators must determine whether the nominee is eligible. To be eligible, a nominee must either be currently employed as a GA/TA at the University of Windsor, or have been employed as a GA/TA at the University of Windsor within 12 months of the call for nominations. The nominee cannot have previously won the award for which he or she is being nominated (though a nominee who has won a *different* award is still eligible). Group nominations are permitted, though in practice it is much more difficult to create an effective nomination dossier for a group, as the dossier must demonstrate that nominees work together as an integrated, collaborative, and coherent team. Three groups have won to date, two of them groups of undergraduate teaching assistants—despite faculty objections that undergraduate TAs were incapable of working at the level that the awards required. We heard these objections frequently when the award processes were being designed, in one-on-one consultations with faculty members, and through email correspondence. We do not hear them now.

Second, the nominators complete the nomination form. Nominators must be *at least two of*: a past or present student of the GA/TA; a colleague, faculty member, or a staff member, each of whom must be well informed of the nominee's teaching excellence or educational leadership. Self-nominations are not permitted. Despite resistance from some faculty members, the odds of a truly excellent teacher who meets the award criteria not having a willing nominator strike us as low, since there are five possible categories from which a nominator could be drawn. Completed nomination forms must be submitted to the Centre for Teaching and Learning and signed by the nominee, the nominators, and a relevant faculty supervisor, department head, or dean. We want to ensure that faculty members are aware that their GA/TAs are being nominated for the award—so they can support them and voice any concerns early in the process, and because making faculty members aware in this way helps us publicize the existence of the awards.

Third, the nominators and nominee, with the assistance of the committee chair (recommended but not required), create a nomination dossier. After the program's first year, the requirements for the nomination dossier were refined to help staff focus on relevant work and prevent the adjudication committee from collapsing due to time pressures. Assessing dossiers takes time, as anyone who has ever assessed one for awards, courses, programs, or hiring will know. Thus, we thought it prudent to take steps to minimize the time investment and make it more efficient by instituting some requirements and limitations. Now, nomination dossiers must be no longer than 40 pages, including letters and appendices; well-organized and readable; and primarily textual, though where appropriate, a CD or DVD of supplementary material may be included, provided that any video or audio is no more than 15 minutes in length, combined, and is playable on multiple hardware formats using common software. The last requirement proved to be quite important, as format compatibility interfered with the adjudication process on several occasions. For this reason, in 2013 we hope to switch to an electronic submission process using e-portfolio software. Nomination dossiers are required to include the following documents:

- The completed **nomination form**
- A **cover letter** from the nominators that explains why the nominee should win the award, providing concrete and relevant examples of what the nominee has done to meet the award criteria, and situating the nominee's work in the context of his/her disciplinary and departmental norms.
- A **curriculum vitae** of 2-8 pages, focusing on details regarding the nominee's teaching experience (including, but not limited to, GA/TA work).
- A **teaching philosophy** (no more than two pages), explaining the nominee's beliefs and values regarding teaching, how those beliefs and values drive his or her teaching practices, and how he or she has developed as a teacher.
- **Letters** (no more than two pages each and no more than six letters total) that detail how the nominee meets the award criteria by making reference to concrete examples and situating the nominee in his or her disciplinary or departmental context. Letters must be from *at least two* current or former students, at least one current or former faculty supervisor, *at least one* GA/TA colleague or staff member detailing how the nominee meets the award criteria.
- **Formal and informal feedback** from students, colleagues, faculty, or staff regarding the nominee's teaching—such as a summary of student evaluations, classroom observation reports, and unsolicited student letters or emails. These should be organized and summarized rather than presented raw.

- **Evidence** of:
  - Reflective and intentional effort to develop teaching knowledge and skills—i.e. through participation in a teaching certificate program, workshops, credit or non-credit courses, seminars, conferences, learning communities, or independent study.
  - Achievements relevant to the award criteria, including but not limited to: examples of exemplary constructive, written, feedback given to students; records of previous teaching awards won; samples of materials prepared to aid student learning; abstracts of presentations and publications on teaching and learning; and any other documentary evidence demonstrating that the nominee has had a positive influence on student learning, retention, or degree completion.

In accordance with Sorcinelli and Gross Davis's (1996) second recommendation for improving teaching awards, not only is evidence solicited from multiple parties, but the committee itself is composed of representatives from across the campus community. Nomination dossiers are reviewed by a committee comprised of a chair from the Centre for Teaching and Learning (non-voting except as a tie-breaker); three faculty members that, as a group, represent a broad range of GA/TA responsibilities; and three GA/TAs (past award winners when possible). The Chair attempts to recruit committee members from as diverse a range of departments and faculties as possible, to maximize the likelihood that the committee is well-informed about the norms for GA/TAs in different areas, and to avoid the possibility that any decision be perceived as unfair to any area.

Prior to the committee's meeting, each member receives a copy of each nomination dossier and a scoring rubric based on the award criteria. Members review and score each dossier individually before the committee meets. After reviewing and discussing each nomination at the meeting, changes in scores are made if necessary, and decisions are made on the basis of those scores. Scores are to be based exclusively on the award criteria, in order to ensure that the purposes of the awards are honoured and that relevant factors are not lost due to biases or individual agendas (Leverenz & Goodburn, 1998). Feedback is solicited for each dossier, to be shared later with nominees.

Once decisions have been made at the meeting, all nominees and their nominators are contacted by email. Each is told whether he/she has won and is provided with constructive feedback based on the committee's discussion, acknowledging positive elements of their dossier, and noting areas for further development. Those who do not win are advised to take the committee's feedback to heart and try again next year.

Winners are announced in the University's Daily News and on the CTL website. Letters of congratulations are sent to each winner's nominators, department head, and faculty dean, in case the latter two wish to follow up with their own form of recognition. Budget constraints (indeed, annual budget cuts) prevent us from offering cash prizes, though winners receive a framed certificate at the annual Celebration of Teaching Excellence, free registration at the next regional teaching and learning conference, and a copy of a teaching related book such as Wilbert McKeachie's *Teaching Tips*. Brief biographies and photos of all winners, including summaries of the accomplishments that resulted in their awards, are featured on the CTL website for future recognition and inspiration.

To further highlight the excellent practices of our award winners, while helping them develop their teaching abilities, most winners are asked to volunteer as facilitators for our GA/TA induction event (GATAcademy) and/or become departmental representatives and facilitators in our GA/TA Network, a collaborative venture with the Faculty of Graduate Studies. This is consistent with Sorcinelli and Gross Davis's (1996) third recommendation for improving teaching awards. In the future, we may explore the option of requiring winners to make public presentations or lead workshops on their practices, as recommended by Jones (2003).

Conclusion

Despite initial misgivings, in our experience, it is possible to create teaching awards that encourage and facilitate meaningful educational development, call attention to the products and performances and processes of effective scholarly teaching, and contribute to cultural change. They can reinforce what we teach graduate students about scholarly and effective teaching by publicly rewarding those who take those notions seriously. They can make individuals aware of scholarly and effective teaching practices in the implicit message behind their criteria and processes—in what is honoured.

Following Chism (2006), we would not recommend relying solely on such awards to accomplish any of the goals listed above. Nevertheless, and although the goals are long-range and progress will be slow, graduate student teaching award programs can be a viable component of a multifaceted strategy that includes consultations, courses, practica, a multifaceted teaching evaluation system, and other programs of depth and complexity.

References

Carraccio, C., & Englander, R. (2004). Evaluating competence using a portfolio: A literature review and web-based application to the ACGME competencies. *Teaching and Learning in Medicine, 16(4)*, 381–387.

Chism, N.V.N. (2006). Teaching awards: What do they award? *The Journal of Higher Education, 77(4)*, 589–617.

Jones, S. (2003). Measuring the quality of higher education: Linking teaching quality measures at the delivery level to administrative measures at the university level. *Quality in higher education, 9(3),* 223–229.

Knapper, C., & Wilcox, S. (2007). Preparing a teaching dossier. Centre for Teaching and Learning: Queen's University.

Knapper, C., & Wright, W.A. (2001). Using portfolios to document good teaching: Premises, purposes, practices. *New Directions for Teaching and Learning, 88,* 19–29.

Leverenz, C.S., & Goodburn, A. (1998). Professionalizing TA training: Commitment to teaching or rhetorical response to market crisis? *Faculty publications – Department of English.* Paper 11. Retrieved from http://digitalcommons.unl.edu/englishfacpubs/11.

Potter, M. K., & Kustra, E. (2011). The Relationship between scholarly teaching and SoTL: Models, distinctions, and clarifications. *International Journal for the Scholarship of Teaching and Learning 5(1).*

Sorcinelli, M.D., & Gross Davis, B. (1996). Honoring exemplary teaching in research universities. *New Directions for Teaching and Learning, 65,* 71–76.

Betsy Keating is an educational developer at the University of Windsor, specializing in teaching assistant and graduate student development in pedagogical practice. She is part of the development team for the University's GA/TA Network, a multi-faceted program for training, support resources, and learning community opportunities.

Michael K. Potter is a teaching and learning specialist and administrator of the University Teaching Certificate Program at the University of Windsor, and coordinator of the GA/TA Awards Program.

Chapter 4
Using Teaching Portfolios in Graduate Teaching Award Nominations

Stephanie V. Rohdieck, Kathryn E. Linder, Dawn Walts, Christina Holmes, & Kathleen M. Hallihan

The authors address three main themes from data collected about the use of teaching portfolios in a TA teaching award process: the representativeness of teaching portfolios; their use for simultaneous summative and formative purposes; and the varied benefits of portfolio development for personal reflection, increased professional development, and job market preparation.

Though many universities that employ graduate students as teaching assistants (TAs) to teach undergraduate courses have some form of teaching award or recognition, there is little existing scholarship on TA teaching awards in the United States. The authors found only two studies that discuss TA awards specifically (Langford, 1987; Willingham-McLain & Pollack, 2006). This literature indicates that teaching portfolios are a required component of the award application, however, the effectiveness of the use of those portfolios for both the award selection process and the award nominees' professionalization has yet to be addressed. This study, conducted at The Ohio State University, which is one of the largest employers of graduate teaching assistants in the U.S. (approximately 2,500 out of a total graduate student population of over 10,000), examines the impact of teaching portfolios in the teaching award process as determinants of teaching effectiveness and as a professional development tool for the award nominees.

This article begins with a description of the Graduate Associate Teaching Award (GATA) and the history of the involvement of the University Center for the Advancement of Teaching (UCAT) in the award process. Following this, we contextualize our research questions with a brief literature review of the purpose of teaching portfolios, benefits and drawbacks of using portfolios as teaching award applications, and some of the recent critiques of their use. Using data collected over five years, we address three main themes that emerge in response to the literature: (1) how well nominees felt teaching portfolios represented their teaching (or 'them as teachers'), (2) the use of portfolios as a simultaneous summative and formative assessment of one's teaching, and (3) the varied benefits of teaching portfolio construction including opportunities for reflection, increased professional development, and additional preparation for the academic job market. We conclude with a discussion of the larger implications of our data and point to areas for future research.

Background of the TA Teaching Award

The Ohio State University, through the Graduate School, has recognized excellence in graduate student teaching since 1973. The Graduate Associate Teaching Award (GATA) is the university's highest recognition of the exceptional teaching provided by graduate students. Open to all disciplines, 10 TAs from across campus are given the GATA every spring term. They receive a $1500 monetary award and a plaque, usually presented by the President or Dean of the Graduate School in a surprise classroom visit. Because the reputation of the award is very high on campus, such recognition is sought by graduate students and the nomination alone is worthy of a citation in one's curriculum vitae. The average number of nominees every year is approximately 120 graduate students at both the masters and doctoral level (about 5% of the total TA population at Ohio State). Most TAs have been nominated for the award by students or faculty, although self-nomination is also allowed. In the original version of the award, once nominated, the TAs had several months to compile a packet of information, including previous student evaluations; the packet of information was intended to help prepare award reviewers for the classroom observation stage.

In the early years, the selection process was heavily weighted on student evaluations and selection committee members' multiple classroom observations of finalists. In 2002, Ohio State's teaching center, The University Center for the Advancement of Teaching (UCAT), became more closely involved in the award process. Through a collaborative effort of the Graduate School and UCAT, the nomination process was revised to include a more robust teaching portfolio (see Table 1) and classroom observations were eliminated. Although most selection committee members found observations helpful, there were many inconsistencies with when and how these were conducted in addition to logistical and work-load challenges. Another limitation was that TAs without teaching assignments during the term in which selection took place were at a disadvantage.

Two main factors influenced the decision to move to a teaching portfolio-based award process. First, based on discussions with Duquesne University's teaching center, we learned of the potential merits of using teaching portfolios in the TA award application process to save on selection committee time and eliminate the inconsistencies with observations, thus leveling the playing field (Willingham-McLain & Pollack, 2006). The Graduate School had also begun to focus more of their efforts toward graduate student professional development. Using the GATA process to incentivize students to learn about and develop teaching portfolios also made the award process useful for the academic job search. In 2004, some students stated that they self-nominated in order to put themselves on a schedule of structured assistance and deadlines so they would have their portfolios ready upon entering the job market. The Graduate School at Ohio State sponsors and coordinates Preparing Future Faculty (PFF), a program with an emphasis on pairing our students with mentors from smaller liberal art schools in Ohio. Graduate student participants in PFF activities often heard liberal arts faculty mention the regular use of teaching portfolios as documents that highlight the importance of reflection in the teaching process and academic job search, which made them realize the importance of preparing for academic interviews.

In 2003, the Graduate School implemented the revised application process. Once the TAs received a nomination, they were provided with guidelines for the portfolio (see Table 1) and were given numerous opportunities to receive assistance creating the documents that comprised their award application. Since that year, UCAT has offered two duplicate 90-minute information sessions several months before the application submission deadline. The UCAT consultant describes each section of the portfolio, shows examples, and discusses tips on

Table 1. Components of the GATA Nominee Portfolio

Component	Description
Description of Teaching Responsibilities	1-2 pages description (no limit on courses, but experience must be from Ohio State)
Summary of Evaluative Feedback	1-2 pages of description and summary of qualitative and quantitative feedback from students, colleagues, and supervisors[a]
Representative Student Evaluations OR Summative Evaluation from One Course	Up to three representative student evaluations OR include cumulative formal evaluation from the university[b]
Teaching Statement	1-2 pages reflection about your personal teaching goals
Instructional Materials	1 teaching artifact with 1 page of explanation and context[c]
Letter of Recommendation	1 letter required from faculty or administrator; one optional letter from a student[d]

Note: Nomination portfolio components changed between 2006 and 2007. Details are below.
[a] In 2004-2006, nominees could provide 1-4 pages of description and evaluative feedback.
[b] In 2004-2006, representative student evaluations and summative course evaluations were not requested.
[c] In 2004-2006, nominees were asked to turn in 2-3 teaching artifacts.
[d] In 2004-2006, nominees did not have the opportunity to include a letter of support from a student.

how each section can be used to demonstrate teaching effectiveness in various disciplines represented by each audience. Each session concludes with answers to questions specific to writing the GATA portfolio.

For the first two years, award nominees resisted the portfolio format and the elimination of the classroom observations. Efforts were made to explain how an observation with no context (which a portfolio could provide) is not an accurate measurement of teaching effectiveness. This initial resistance to the changes was likely based on the fact that some of these nominees had been nominated and observed previously under the former system. By 2006, resistance from nominees lessened significantly, particularly during the question and answer portion of the nominee portfolio information sessions.

Research Questions and Methodology

Given the significant changes made to the award process, the Graduate School and UCAT recognized the importance of gathering data to assess the impact of the changes. Direct and indirect data were collected and analyzed to inform future changes in an ongoing systematic way. From 2004 through 2008, yearly data was compiled and assessed and the application portfolio requirements were modified accordingly. The authors were interested in accessing this data in order to answer the following questions:

1. Do GATA nominees believe their teaching portfolios will provide the selection committee with adequate evidence of the quality of their teaching?
2. What additional value (beyond the potential to win an award), if any, do GATA nominees perceive in creating a teaching portfolio?
   - Do they perceive it to be a useful part of their own professional development as a teacher?
   - Do they perceive it to be a valuable part of their career preparation efforts?

The analysis of answers to the above questions shed light on the utility of teaching portfolios for graduate students at our university and also contributes to the field by highlighting as yet unstudied benefits that portfolio preparation offers for the professionalization of students.

To assess the format changes internally in 2004, the Graduate School, with the help of UCAT, began surveying nominees through the online survey tool Zoomerang. Because the survey was anonymous and no identifying information (such as department affiliation) was asked of respondents, the data set is somewhat limited. This issue is addressed later in this article. The survey was distributed by email to the entire population of award nominees (n=579) each spring for years 2004 to 2008. The survey invitation went out a few weeks after the portfolios were due to the Graduate School, and the survey closed before winners of the award were announced each spring. In those five years, a total

of 266 responses to the survey (a 45.94% response rate) were aggregated and summarized. Initially, the survey was administered to assess larger questions that are outside the scope of this article. Respondents were asked 26 questions (see Appendix) across a variety of categories in order to gauge the:
- clarity of portfolio instructions and guidelines,
- difficulty of constructing the portfolio,
- time investment for respondents in portfolio construction,
- value of the portfolio for the respondents personally and professionally,
- representativeness of the portfolio to the respondents' teaching,
- resources used when compiling the portfolios,
- respondents' knowledge of the purposes of teaching portfolios, and
- respondents' overall confidence level in creating a teaching portfolio after completing the award nomination process.

All quantitative answers in the survey were based on scales of yes/no or a 1-5 Likert scale. The online survey tool summarized averages and counts for answers to quantitative questions. Content analysis of answers to open-ended, qualitative questions was also completed to identify emerging themes and patterns. Data collection was not consistent in 2005 resulting in lower than expected rates of response (n=8). Relevant quantitative data for respondent ratings of resources was analyzed using SPSS® software. Using an ANOVA multivariate analysis, no statistically significant differences were found between resource ratings across all years, so further data analysis was completed using aggregate data. One exception to this is the web use rating between 2005 and 2006; the difference between this rating was significant at p=0.049. However, due to the small sample size in 2005, we did not consider these results in this publication. All other analyses included data from years 2004-2008 (see Table 2).

Table 2. Number of students nominated, portfolios submissions, and survey responses from 2004-2008

Year	Students Nominated	Portfolio Submissions	Survey Responses
2004	49	32	42
2005	105	88	8
2006	129	86	76
2007	204	72	84
2008	92	50	56
Total	579	328	266[a]

[a] There were 266 total responses to the survey for questions 1, 12-18. There were 236 responses for questions 2-11 because these were only made available when the respondents indicated they submitted a portfolio (question 1).

Emergent Themes from Our Data

There were several emergent themes in the data that furthered our knowledge of the representativeness of portfolios as well as what made the time investment of creating a portfolio worthwhile to the graduate students who participated in the application process. We elaborate on these themes below.

Portfolios as Representative

Over the years some nominees expressed the concern that a teaching portfolio cannot adequately represent someone's teaching effectiveness as well as a classroom observation. Hence, this has been an important question for us. Sixty-three percent (n=149) of the 236 respondents indicating they submitted a portfolio either agreed or strongly agreed with the statement "I feel the GATA nomination portfolio is representative of what I do as a teacher." When asked if the "GATA nomination portfolio structure was flexible enough to adequately represent [their] teaching ability," 56.36% of respondents (n=133) agreed or strongly agreed. Only 2.12% (n=5) strongly disagreed that the portfolio was representative of their teaching and only 21.18% (n=50) believed the structure was not flexible enough to adequately represent their teaching. The relatively strong agreement about the representativeness and flexibility of portfolios may have been influenced by the fact that 80.1% (n=189) of the respondents knew about teaching portfolios before the nomination process. Fifty-three percent (n=125) had created either a complete or partial teaching portfolio prior to their nomination.

Sample Survey Comments on the Representativeness of Portfolios
- "I thought the documents I created were very personal and reflected me as a teacher." (2005)
- "There was room for expression and flexibility to show skills and strengths." (2006)
- "The portfolio represents my teaching approaches well. I found tremendous flexibility. I wanted to include visual aids and was able to do so in the artifacts section." (2007)
- "I believe that the required parts of the portfolio… allowed me to present a range of information about how I teach, thus making it fairly representative of what I do in the classroom." (2008)
- "I think it was flexible enough so that if people were creative and concise they had plenty of space to describe their teaching styles." (2008)

When asked to provide an explanation for their rating on representativeness and flexibility of the nomination portfolio, 160 (67.79%) respondents provided one. Forty-six of those responses (28.75%) were about the lack of representativeness or flexibility in the structure of the portfolio itself, specifically regarding elements of the nomination process that they wish had been included, such as nominee interviews or classroom observations by selection committee members, videotapes of classes, or the inclusion of additional artifacts. We then specifically examined the responses from 2006 and 2007 (n=63) since these nominees had even less flexibility in the portfolio components than those in earlier years (see table 1). Only a few of those respondents commented that the portfolio process did not suit their discipline as well as others (8%, n=5) or that writing a good portfolio does not reflect good teaching (these are 2 different skills) (8%, n=5). Based on these data, a strong case can be made that GATA nominees believe their teaching portfolios provided the selection committee with adequate evidence of the quality of their teaching.

Portfolio Preparation is Worthwhile

An obvious benefit of using teaching portfolios in the award process is that nominees may use them later in their job searches; beyond this utilitarian aim, questions remain about use of portfolios for both formative and summative purposes. For example, there is some question as to whether formative and summative uses of a portfolio can occur simultaneously. De Rijdt, Tiquet, Dochy, and Devolder (2006) imply that a portfolio can either be used for evaluation or reflection but not necessarily both. Tillema and Smith (2000) also make this differentiation when they identify three distinct portfolio formats: dossiers, course-related learning, and reflective portfolios. In particular, they draw a relationship between the kind of portfolio one intends to create and the benefits received from that portfolio including, but not limited to, the type of feedback offered by a reader or reviewer (see also Tillema, 1998). Bunker and Leggett (2004) critique higher education literature for not being explicit enough about teaching portfolio definitions, claiming, "much of the literature and many of the associated practices surrounding tertiary teaching portfolios conflate formative and summative assessment and are disconnected from good practice in assessment" (p. 100). The authors express concern that this lack of definition leads to confusion for creators of teaching portfolios regarding the purpose of its construction.

Our survey results indicate that the GATA nominees who submitted portfolios were not confused about their role or function. In fact, 92.79% (n=219) of respondents agreed that the GATA nomination portfolio preparation process was a "worthwhile," "somewhat worthwhile," or "very worthwhile" endeavor that supported their professional development. The positive response regarding the perceived value of portfolio development increased six percentage points (from 89.57 to 95.87) after there was a change in the format of the portfolio (academic years 2004-2006 versus 2007-2008).

Second, when specifically asked to explain why (or why not) they thought it was worthwhile, respondents (n=163) most frequently indicated they felt it was useful for both summative and formative purposes: their academic job search process (43.56%, n=71) and for reflecting on their teaching (30.06%, n=49). Other less frequently cited comment themes were related to changes made in their teaching or general professional development. We explore these themes in more detail below.

When asked to specifically rate the usefulness of the portfolio for various purposes (see Table 3), respondents chose reflection on teaching more often as a useful purpose than job search preparation. However, those purposes represented 94.07% (n=222) versus 80.93% (n=191) of nominees respectively, clearly indicating that both of these functions are simultaneously useful to them. The third highest rated benefit of the nomination portfolio was to show changes in teaching (71.19%, n=168). It is important to note that the 236 respondents to this question chose 784 responses. Most chose more than one possible answer, clearly indicating that the portfolio addressed multiple needs and could be used simultaneously for multiple purposes, both summative and formative.

Several scholars agree with our respondents that teaching portfolios have value (1) as reflective tools (Border, 2002; Drake & McBride, 2000; Hurst, Wilson, & Cramer, 1998; Knapper & Wright, 2001; Willingham-McLain & Pollack, 2006), (2) as general professional development (Wright, Knight, & Pomerleau, 1999), and (3) for the academic job search process (Drake & McBride, 2000; Willingham-McLain & Pollack, 2006). Below, we offer further evidence of the significance of these three themes to the respondents in our study.

(1) Portfolios as Reflective Tools

Scholars have repeatedly affirmed the reflective benefits of teaching portfolios. Because preparing a teaching portfolio often involves the collecting of one's teaching materials, student evaluations, and peer feedback into a comprehensive

Table 3. Percentage of Positive Responses Regarding the Usefulness of the Nomination Portfolio

Useful for the following reasons	2004	2008	Average across all years
Allowed me to be reflective about my teaching	89% (n=33)	96% (n=47)	94.07% (n=222)
Showed how I've made changes in my teaching	54% (n=20)	82% (n=40)	80.93% (n=191)
Gave me ideas about new teaching techniques	35% (n=13)	49% (n=24)	71.19% (n=168)
Made me think about teaching in a different way	22% (n=8)	55% (n=27)	44.07% (n=104)
Will use it when applying for jobs in academia	84% (n=31)	86% (n=42)	37.71% (n=89)
Other	3% (n=1)	6% (n=3)	4.24% (n=10)

Note: Data were also collected for 2005, 2006 and 2007. N=236 for all years.

report, the portfolio author often engages in a process of self-reflection as he or she brings together artifacts that are regarded as representative of his or her teaching effectiveness (Drake & McBride; Hurst, et. al., 1998, 2000). In situations where portfolio authors are receiving formative feedback, they may be identifying a direct relationship between their portfolio documents and their current teaching practices. Even when used as a part of summative evaluations, portfolio authors may still be asked to reflect on areas of strength and improvement.

Even when the purpose of developing a teaching portfolio is unclear (i.e., whether it is being used for summative or formative feedback, or both) scholars have found that regardless of purpose, "to prepare a persuasive teaching portfolio requires both self-evaluation and reflection about personal teaching goals" (Knapper & Wright, 2001, p. 27). Drake and McBride (2000) have identified three areas of growth for instructors who engage in self-reflection through the creation of a teaching portfolio: growth in the subject one is teaching, growth as an instructor who examines and evaluates pedagogical choices, and growth as a "teacher-scholar" (p. 43) who sees the inherent connection between teaching and learning.

In their article about the use of portfolios in a TA award program, Willingham-McLain and Pollack (2006) discuss the valuable reflection opportunities that portfolios provide, specifically for graduate student instructors. In addition to helping prepare them for the job market, the authors note that the "guided reflection" of the portfolio building process is an advantage for all graduate students, but especially for those graduate student instructors with little teaching experience who need "to develop the habit of reflecting on and improving their teaching" (Willingham-McLain & Pollack, 2006, p. 250). We suggest that even though some of the literature argues that the reward process may compete with the reflection process, our data validates our initial intention of creating an award structure that allows for, and even rewards, thoughtful reflection.

Sample Survey Comments on Reflection
- "It was the first time I was forced to think of my teaching in a structured way." (2004)
- "I think it was definitely worthwhile as it was a really good experience in terms of evaluating my teaching experience over the past few years, as well as good practice in writing a document that effectively presents my teaching theories and why I do what I do." (2006)
- "I've been nominated twice and both times I thought it was very, very worthwhile—I've learned new things I could do… for me, at least, I saw how I had grown and changed as a teacher." (2006)
- "Composing my portfolio made me assess my methods and why it is that I do what I do. It was nice to stop and reflect on my teaching and the areas I need to improve on." (2007)

- "It really made me stop and think about WHY I'm doing what I'm doing, and realize that 'because I saw someone else do it this way' isn't a good enough answer." (2007)

(2) Portfolios as Tools for General Professional Development

Many scholars have written about the numerous benefits of creating a teaching portfolio for one's general professional development. Ouellette (2007) states that the teaching portfolio can help individuals contextualize their teaching within other professional responsibilities. Importantly, scholars have found that not only do portfolio authors reflect on their own teaching, but often they are also placing their teaching in relation to their larger role within the academy. Indeed, Wright and Pomerleau in their 1999 study on the use of portfolios in higher education found, "when teachers keep portfolios, they reflect on their own goals and practices and regularly have to examine the fit of their goals with other views of the academy and the fit of their teaching and evaluation practices with their goals" (p. 100). For graduate students in particular, reflecting on teaching through a portfolio allows them to develop, as indicated by Hutchings (1998), "a conception of teaching as scholarly, intellectual work" (p. 239).

In addition to helping graduate students explore how teaching fits into their views of the academy and how the portfolio writing process allows for socialization into the academy (Hutchings, 1998), there are other immediate ways a portfolio contributes to one's professional development. As Ouellett (2007) states, a portfolio helps instructors see patterns in their teaching over time, as well as evolutions and growth they may have had a as teacher. It helps instructors recognize their strengths and weaknesses as a teacher (see also Drake & McBride, 2000). With that recognition comes confidence in one's teaching abilities and working to improve them (Smith & Tillema, 2001) as well as "quality control" (Hutchings, 1998, p. 240). And finally, portfolios allow instructors to "be in control of the direction of personal learning" (Smith & Tillema, 2001, p. 183).

As the following comments indicate, the nominees for our teaching award had many insights into the usefulness of the portfolio writing process to their own teaching development.

Sample Survey Comments on General Professional Development

- "I actually see better, after completing this portfolio, what I have to do next and where I stand." (2004)
- "Teaching is something I plan on doing for my entire career, and building this portfolio gave me a foundation to build upon." (2006)
- "It made me reevaluate WHAT I was doing in my classroom, and HOW I was doing it. I think it enhanced my teaching and made me much clearer about some things I've been doing intuitively." (2006)

- "I have implemented many new aspects to my teaching that seem to integrate more functionality and this stemmed from my focus on analyzing my teaching for the portfolio." (2008)

Interestingly, one area that these scholars have not considered in depth is the usefulness of the portfolio for the professional development of those not planning a career as a teacher. Several of our respondents who identified as master's or doctoral students whose career plans will take them outside of higher education nonetheless answered that they believed the portfolios to be useful to their professional development. For example, one respondent commented, "While I am not going to continue on as a teacher, it did help me re-affirm my abilities to teach a new skill to others (which can be useful in the working world and pretty much anywhere)." Another wrote, "It would be very helpful because it shows how much leadership I have in doing my job." Our survey did not include a specific question on future career aspirations, as this was not the initial focus of the study. The qualitative data we found suggests an avenue for future research on this topic.

(3) Portfolios as Tools for the Job search

A third area where scholars have identified the benefits of creating a teaching portfolio is in the job search process. Willingham-McLain and Pollack (2006), in particular, note how graduate students can simultaneously reflect on their teaching and practice while developing materials they may need in their career preparation. Moreover, Border (2002) notes that the process of creating the portfolio and the self-reflection involved allows students "to be articulate and convincing in their oral interviews" (p. 742). The benefits of the portfolio to the interview process are also noted by Meizlish and Kaplan (2006) who argue that interviewees with "concrete evidence of teaching experience" rather than "vague platitudes," (p. 501) are more highly valued on the job market.

Meizlish and Kaplan (2006) also note that teaching statements, a foundational component of a teaching portfolio, are the most commonly requested document. Although they found that a small percentage of institutions asked for a complete portfolio, they found that 57% of the hiring institutions they surveyed asked for teaching statements later in the interview process. Although Schonwetter, Taylor and Ellis (2006) found that only 5% of U.S. schools asked for full portfolios in job advertisements, both Hutchings (1998) and Drake and McBride (2000) have noted the benefit of the teaching portfolio creation process to the applicants' level of confidence while on the job market. Specifically, Hutchings notes that having materials helps students on the job market be better prepared to talk about their teaching experience.

The data from the award nominees in our study are consistent with the literature regarding the academic job search.

Sample Survey Comments on the Job Search
- "I will need a teaching portfolio when I go on the job market a year from now, so this was a good start. It also made me rethink some of my teaching practices and implement new ideas, like mid-quarter evaluations." (2004)
- "We do not support teaching in my department and this was helpful in preparing me for the job market as I wish to be a Professor and teaching is a major focus of mine." (2005)
- "I feel these materials will be invaluable in the job search process. I am glad to begin creating and editing these documents." (2006)
- "I am so glad to have had this opportunity because I will DEFINITELY use these materials next year on the job market." (2007)
- "As someone who plans on being an academic once I complete my PhD, I need to have a portfolio put together before applying for jobs next year. Doing that for the GATA puts me a step ahead of where I would normally be." (2008)

Mentorship for Portfolio Preparation and Reflection

One final piece of evidence from our data that fits into the scope of this article supports the current literature on TA mentorship. One method for combating the lack of definition and conflation of the summative and formative purposes of a teaching portfolio (Bunker & Leggett, 2004) is the encouragement of mentorship within the portfolio creation process. For example, Border (2002) emphasizes the importance of dialogue between graduate student portfolio authors and faculty. These mentors "should be aware of the job market, appreciative of different post-secondary cultures, up to date on current trends in graduate education, and informed about graduate programs" (Border, 2002, p. 741). For this award process, we offered our nominees numerous opportunities to receive this guidance. We directly asked award nominees to characterize the kind of mentorship they received while building their portfolios (see Table 4).

A large majority of the 266 respondents participated in the resources available to them. Each year we offered two well-attended (58.97%, n=161) identical workshops where UCAT and Graduate School staff described and answered questions about the nomination portfolio components. UCAT staff then facilitated a workshop on developing a teaching portfolio, with emphasis on the parts relevant to the GATA portfolio. The workshop participation rates varied throughout the five years of the study with a low of 52% (n=75) in 2006 and a high of 70.73% (n=41) in 2004. Respondents reported using the online materials from the workshops (63.04%, n=162) and those handed out during and after the sessions (70.87%, n=180), which included supplemental examples and guiding questions. There was a consistent reliance on outside help with a 5-year use rate of 40.94% (n=104). Those that commented on getting outside help mentioned using the following resources for portfolio development: former GATA winners, advisors, peers, TA Coordinators, and non-teaching center websites.

Individual consultations by UCAT staff had the highest value rating of all of the teaching center resources provided (average rating=4.32 on a scale of 1-5, 1=no value at all, 3=valuable, 5=extremely valuable). The confidential consultations provide nominees with individualized feedback on their portfolio drafts and engage them in reflective discussion about their portfolios and teaching practices. The reliance on individual consultations rose steadily over the five years of the study; 2004 had a use rate of 31.71% (n=41) and 2008 had a use rate of 64.81% (n=54). This increase may be attributed to changes in the GATA nomination portfolio format in 2007. With those changes, it became easier for nominees to sign-up online for teaching center individual consultations; we also worked with the Graduate School to advertise these free services.

For those GATA nominees who considered self-reflection to be an important element of building a teaching portfolio, individual consultations provided the most helpful mentorship. To determine if there was a relationship between mentorship and self-reflection, we looked through all records to verify if the respondent wrote anywhere in the survey about the importance of reflection, and then we traced the types of mentoring interactions they indicated they had experienced. Out of the 60 respondents (25.42%) writing about reflection, 75% of them (n=45) rated consultations with UCAT staff as either valuable, very valuable, or extremely valuable. Across all years, the individual consultations received more ratings of "extremely valuable" than any other service or resource offered.

Border's (2002) argument that portfolio creation benefits from mentorship appears to be true for the GATA nominees in our study. A large number of them used one or more resources to assist them in creating their portfolios, and

Table 4. Use and Perceived Value of Resources for Creating GATA Nominee Teaching Portfolios (2004-2008)

	Portfolio Workshop[a]	Individual Consultation[a]	On line Materials[a]	Workshop Materials[a]	Outside of UCAT
Use of resource	58.97%	47.49%	63.04%	70.87%	40.94%
Value of resource	4.05	4.32	3.94	3.91	4.09
N	161	123	162	180	104
N[b]	261	259	257	254	254

Note: Values are mean scores on a 5-point scale (1 = no value whatsoever, 3 = valuable, 5 = extremely valuable). N=266. Respondents could provide an answer to more than one resource.
[a]Resources were provided by staff in UCAT, Ohio State's teaching center.
[b]There were 266 respondents to the survey. Not every respondent answered the questions.

for all of these resources across all years, respondents rated them as valuable; the lowest average score was 4.39 (n=13) in 2004 and the highest average was 4.67 in 2006. The individual consultation was clearly a valuable process for respondents, particularly in helping them self-reflect on their teaching.

Conclusion

Our data shows that teaching centers can serve an important, and perhaps foundational, role in supporting teaching award processes for graduate students. As evidenced by comments from nominees regarding the support they received from UCAT, the mentorship received in one-on-one consultation sessions was the most helpful aspect to the reflective development process. The collaboration between the Graduate School and UCAT highlights one successful model that is not only beneficial in terms of resource sharing at the institutional level, but most importantly, is seen as beneficial by the graduate students themselves.

The research methods and findings presented above are significant because they address a major gap in the scholarly literature: lack of formal studies and/or controlled experiments that support (or refute) claims of the benefits of teaching portfolios in higher education (Burns, 1999 and 2000.) This article not only presents quantitative and qualitative methods, but the findings validate multiple benefits of teaching portfolio development, as well as the importance of mentoring. The large amount of data collected for our study implies a relationship between teaching portfolios and positive changes in the classroom, a research topic worthy of further investigation. In addition, the successful data-driven changes made in the award process during the time span of the study resulted in a solidification of the use of teaching portfolios in both the TA teaching award and graduate student professional development process.

The goals of this study were threefold: (1) to determine if those creating the teaching portfolios viewed it as an adequate representation of their teaching for the purposes of the award; (2) to measure the perceived value of the creation of a teaching portfolio as academic career preparation; and (3) to gauge the perceived value of the creation of a teaching portfolio in terms of professional development not related to academic career development. Based on the analysis of respondent data over five years, it is our conclusion that respondents felt the portfolio was representative of their teaching and that they found great value in creating one, especially with reference to academic job preparation but also as preparation for other careers. There was no indication that there was tension, much less opposition, between the summative and formative purposes of the portfolios. In fact, the data illustrates the contrary, namely that the two purposes, from the viewpoint of the portfolio creators, at worst went unnoticed and at best enhanced each other.

Based on our study, additional research on the use of teaching portfolios in the teaching award process could include the impact of that process for faculty as well as disciplinary differences in portfolio preparation. Further exploration about the benefits of portfolios for graduate students that pursue non-academic jobs is also needed. A study on how selection committees use the judging criteria when scoring teaching portfolios for a TA teaching award is found in chapter 7 of this volume.

References

Border, L. (2002). The Socratic portfolio: a guide for future faculty. *PS: Political Science and Politics, 35*(4), 739–742.

Bunker, A., & Leggett, M. (2004). Being wise about teaching portfolios: exploring the barriers to their development and maintenance. *HERDSA: Research & Development in Higher Education Series* (pp. 92–101).

Burns, C. W. (1999). Teaching portfolios and the evaluation of teaching in higher education: confident claims, questionable research support. *Studies in Educational Evaluation, 25,* 131–142.

Burns, C. W. (2000). Teaching portfolios: another perspective. *Academe, 86*(1), 44–47.

De Rijdt, C. Tiquet, E., Dochy, F., & Devolder, M. (2006). Teahing portfolios in higher education and their effects: an explorative study. *Teaching and Teacher Education, 22,* 1084–1093.

Drake, F. D., & McBride, L. W. (2000). The summative teaching portfolio and the reflective practitioner of history. *The History Teacher, 34*(1), 41–60.

Hurst, B., Wilson, C., & Cramer, G. (1998). Professional teaching portfolios: tools for reflection, growth, and advancement. *The Phi Delta Kappan, 79*(8), 578–582.

Hutchings, P. (1998). Teaching portfolios as a tool for TA development. In Marincovich, M., et al. (Eds.), *The Professional Development of Graduate Teaching Assistants* (pp. 235–248). Bolton: MA: Anker Publishing.

Knapper, C., & Wright, W. A. (2001). Using portfolios to document good teaching: premises, purposes, practices. In C. Knapper & P. Cranton (Eds.), *New Directions in Teaching and Learning: No. 88. Fresh approaches to the evaluation of teaching* (pp. 19–29). San Francisco, CA: Jossey-Bass.

Langford, T. A. (1987). Recognizing outstanding teaching. In N. V. N. Chism (Ed.), *Institutional responsibilities and responses in employment and education of teaching assistants: readings from a national conference* (pp. 132–133). The Ohio State University: Center for Teaching Excellence.

Meizlish, D., & and Kaplan, M. (2008). Valuing and evaluating teaching in academic hiring: a multidisciplinary, cross-institutional study. *The Journal of Higher Education, 79*(5),489–512.

Ouellett, M. L. (2007). Your teaching portfolio: strategies for initiating and documenting growth and development. *Journal of Management Education, 31*(3), 421–433.

Schönwetter, Dieter J. (2006). Reading the want ads: how can current job descriptions inform professional development programs for graduate students? *Journal on Excellence in College Teaching, 17,* 159–188.

Smith, K., & and Tilemma, H. H. (2001). Long-term influences of portfolios on professional development. *Scandinavian Journal of Educational Research, 45*(2), 183–203.

Tillema, H. H. (1998). Design and validity of a portfolio instrument for professional training. *Studies in Educational Evaluation, 24*(3), 263–278.

Tillema, H. H., & Smith, K. (2000). Learning from portfolios: differential use of feedback in portfolio construction. *Studies in Educational Evaluation, 26*, 193–210.

Willingham-McLain, L., & Pollack, D. (2006). Exploring the application of best practices to TA awards: one university's approach. In S. Chadwick-Blossey & D.R. Robertson (Eds.), *To Improve the Academy: Vol. 24. Resources for Faculty, Instructional, and Organizational Development* (pp. 247–258). Bolton, MA: Anker.

Wright, A. W., Knight, P. T., & Pomerleau, N. (1999). Portfolio people: teaching and learning dossiers and innovation in higher education. *Innovative Higher Education, 24*(2), 89–103.

Stephanie V. Rohdieck is the Associate Director of the University Center for the Advancement of Teaching at The Ohio State University. She teaches courses on college teaching and teaching support for graduate teaching assistants. Her current research interests are graduate teaching preparation, teaching portfolio development, diversity, teaching awards, clinical teaching, and instructional consultation.

Kathryn E. Linder is the Director of the Center for Teaching and Scholarly Excellence at Suffolk University in Boston. Her current research interests include blended course design, scholarly writing productivity, and faculty development. Most recently, she is the author of *Rampage Violence Narratives: What Fictional Accounts of School Shootings Say about the Future of America's Youth* (Lexington Press, 2014).

Dawn Walts is an Assistant Professor of English at Lewis University. She specializes in Medieval Literature, Shakespeare, and First-Year Writing. She was a recipient of the Graduate Associate Teaching Award at The Ohio State University in 2005.

Christy Holmes is an Assistant Professor of Women's Studies at DePauw University. Her research and teaching interests bridge environmental, transnational, and Chicana feminisms. She also plays an active role in faculty development at the university and has published on strategies to introduce transnational feminist pedagogy in the U.S. classroom.

Kathleen M. Hallihan is the Director of Admissions and Student Services for the John Glenn School of Public Affairs at The Ohio State University. She teaches courses on college teaching and specializes in academic strategic planning, program assessment and accreditation at all levels. She is an accreditor with the Western Association of Schools and Colleges, and is the advisor for co-curricular programs such as the Ohio Student Education Policy Institute. She directed the Preparing Future Faculty Program at Ohio State from 2004-2007.

Appendix A
Survey on the Graduate Associate Teaching Award (GATA) Nomination Process
The Ohio State University

Congratulations on being nominated for a Graduate Associate Teaching Award (GATA). This is a wonderful honor! This year, only (# of nominees) TAs were nominated out of a graduate teaching population of over 2500. The Graduate School and UCAT are interested in knowing about your experience with the GATA process, whether or not you chose to submit an application portfolio. Your feedback is invaluable to us, and we use it every year to improve the process for students. Your participation in this survey is anonymous (no identifying information will be asked of you) and data collected cannot be linked to any specific individual. We anticipate this survey taking approximately 15-20 minutes to complete. If you have any questions or concerns about this survey, please contact (contact person). Thank you!

1. Did you submit a GATA nomination portfolio?

    ☐ Yes
    ☐ No

    If you answered Yes to Question 1 please answer the following questions. If you answered NO to Question 1 please go to Question 12.

The following set of questions pertains to the GATA nomination portfolio you developed.

2. Please rate the usefulness of the instructions for developing the GATA nomination portfolio. (1= strongly disagree, 3=neutral, 5=strongly agree)

    1 2 3 4 5   The guidelines provided sufficient instruction regarding the materials to be included in the GATA nomination portfolio.

    1 2 3 4 5   The GATA nomination portfolio formatting requirements were clear.

    1 2 3 4 5   The instructions provided clear explanation of the criteria to be used in the evaluation process.

3. Approximately how long did it take you to develop the GATA nomination portfolio?

　　☐ 5 hours or fewer
　　☐ 6-10
　　☐ 11-15
　　☐ 16-20
　　☐ 21-25
　　☐ More than 25

4. What was the difficulty level in putting the GATA nomination portfolio together?
1 2 3 4 5 (1=not at all difficult, 3=moderately difficult, 5=extremely difficult)

5. Why did you rate it that way?

6. Please answer the following questions regarding your GATA nomination portfolio. (1= strongly disagree, 3=neutral, 5=strongly agree)

　　☐ I feel the GATA nomination portfolio is representative of what I do as a teacher.
　　☐ The GATA nomination portfolio structure was flexible enough to adequately represent my teaching ability.

7. Why did you respond as you did to Question 6?

8. How worthwhile was the GATA nomination portfolio preparation process to your own professional development?
1 2 3 4 5 (1=Not worthwhile at all, 3=Worthwhile, 5=Very worthwhile)

9. Why did you respond as you did to Question 8?

10. Do you believe the process of putting together a GATA nomination portfolio was useful to you in any of the following ways? (Please check all that apply)

　　☐ Allowed me to be reflective about my teaching.
　　☐ Showed how I've made changes in my teaching.
　　☐ Gave me ideas about new teaching techniques.
　　☐ Made me think about teaching in a different way.
　　☐ Will use it when applying for jobs in academic.
　　☐ Other, please specify

11. What recommendations or suggestions do you have to improve the GATA nomination process for future competitions?

The following section pertains to resources you may have used in developing your GATA nomination portfolio.

12. Please rate the value of any of the following services/resources you may have used in developing your GATA nomination portfolio. Select N/A if you did not use the particular resource. (1=No value whatsoever, 3=valuable, 5=extremely valuable)

    1 2 3 4 5 The UCAT workshop titled "Developing your GATA Nomination Portfolio"
    1 2 3 4 5 An individual consultation with a UCAT consultant
    1 2 3 4 5 The UCAT Teaching Portfolio web site
    1 2 3 4 5 The materials provided to me by UCAT
    1 2 3 4 5 Assistance received form someone outside UCAT

    For each item above there was a follow-up question: Why did you rate it that way?

13. Do you have any additional comments on any aspect of the GATA nomination process?

The following set of questions pertains to teaching portfolios.

14. Please answer the following questions using Yes or No

    Prior to the GATA nomination process, had you ever heard of a teaching portfolio?
    ☐ Yes
    ☐ No
    Have you ever written a teaching portfolio (or parts of one) in the past?
    ☐ Yes
    ☐ No

15. Are you planning on developing a teaching portfolio in the future?
    ☐ Yes   If yes, why and for what purposes?
    ☐ No

16. How confident are you in developing a teaching portfolio?
    1 2 3 4 5   (1=not confident at all, 3=confident, 5=very confident)

17. How likely are you to seek assistance from UCAT in developing your teaching portfolio in the future?
    1 2 3 4 5   (1=not likely at all, 3=likely, 5=very likely)

18. For what reasons do you think people develop teaching portfolios (please check all that apply)?*
    - ☐ Gathering evidence about ones teaching effectiveness
    - ☐ Presenting specific data about ones teaching
    - ☐ Providing structure for self-reflection about areas that need improvement
    - ☐ Fostering an academic environment where discussions about teaching becomes the norm
    - ☐ Applying for teaching awards
    - ☐ Presenting documentation to be submitted in a job search
    - ☐ Other, please specify

* This list was adapted from Seldin, P. (2003). The *Teaching Portfolio*, 3rd ed. San Francisco: Jossey-Bass.

Chapter 5
Building Reflective Practitioners: The Benefit of Awarding Teaching Portfolio Development

Allison Boye, Suzanne Tapp, & Micah Meixner Logan

This paper examines the significance of a teaching portfolio award in a graduate student development program. Fellows acknowledged for outstanding portfolios report gaining confidence in their dossiers and in their teaching as a result of the reflective and evaluative processes, as well as assistance on the job market. In addition, we describe the portfolio development process, evaluation, and selection process.

Teaching portfolios are an effective and tangible process to help faculty members and teachers who wish to compile information about themselves and reflect on the "what, how and why" of their teaching. While much has been written about the creation of portfolios (Murray, 1994; Seldin, Miller, & Seldin, 2010; Wolf & Dietz, 1998), little has been said about recognizing excellence in portfolio development. Sorcinelli and Davis (1996) note that teaching awards are particularly effective as an incentive that encourage faculty members toward continued effort and devotion to one's craft. But do teaching awards for graduate students serve a larger purpose in helping our future faculty members enter the professoriate with more assurance and insight into their own teaching practice? Fellows in our program acknowledged for their outstanding portfolios and, more importantly, for the developmental process and reflection undertaken in the creation of their portfolios, consistently report that the benefit of this recognition is, in a word, confidence. The value of the creative and reflective portfolio process and the effect of teaching awards on the job search were also benefits noted by our Fellows. It seems intuitive then to suggest that a graduate student development program emphasizing teaching portfolios, and recognizing the work put into the development of those portfolios, ultimately benefits the professoriate on a larger scale as we build future faculty members who are ultimately more reflective practitioners as a result of these experiences.

An Overview of the TEACH Program

The Teaching Effectiveness And Career enHancement (TEACH) Program at the Teaching, Learning, and Professional Development Center of Texas Tech University is an adaptation of the Preparing Future Faculty movement (http://www.preparing-faculty.org/) and is specifically designed for PhD or terminal Master's degree students interested in a career in academe. The TEACH Program is well established and has gained a national reputation over the past ten years.

Fellows are recommended by faculty members and selected through a competitive process based on either merit (good teachers who could become excellent) or need (teachers who have faced challenges and stand to benefit from focused time on their teaching). Fellows are paired with a faculty development consultant to focus on teaching effectiveness through observations and feedback, and a faculty mentor relationship is established to offer additional perspectives. In both the fall and spring semesters, TEACH Fellows engage in a videotaped observation of their classes as well as a small-group instructional diagnosis (SGID), a well-known format of anonymous mid-term evaluation conducted by program consultants (Clark & Redmond, 1982).

Our Fellows also participate in 20 hours of teaching and learning workshops offered by our center and attended by faculty members from all ranks and disciplines. Our sessions are informal, interactive, and practical, geared toward ideas that cross disciplines, and designed to maintain our center's mission of supporting teaching effectiveness.

Finally, Fellows are required to complete a teaching portfolio and carry out a Scholarship of Teaching and Learning (SoTL) project of their choice. The process of completing a portfolio engages the Fellows in reflection and asks them to consider whether they are teaching the way they want to teach. The project is a way to get Fellows involved in SoTL research early in their careers and help them realize the value of examining teaching with a scholarly lens. While TEACH Fellows respond positively to every element of the program, the teaching portfolio is one element that they routinely find extremely beneficial, both in terms of development and practical career purposes.

Teaching Portfolio Development

Recognizing the importance of a well-constructed teaching portfolio as well as the significance of clearly communicated expectations and requirements in any recognition process (Chism, 2006; Menges, 1996), the faculty development consultants at our center strive to provide graduate students with the resources necessary for them to develop a strong portfolio. As many graduate students are unfamiliar with the idea of a teaching portfolio, one of the most essential workshops we offer is *Creating Your Teaching Portfolio*, based on the work of Peter Seldin (2004). In this workshop, which we offer multiple times throughout the year, an experienced faculty developer presents various components of a teaching portfolio as well as discipline specific practices and expectations. One unique feature of this workshop is that the main focus of the time is spent in a hands-on examination of portfolios collected over the years from past TEACH Fellows.

Another document that plays a critical role in the development of a strong teaching portfolio and job application packet is the teaching philosophy statement. Many institutions require applicants to submit a teaching philosophy statement, and this is an undeniably difficult document to write (Montell, 2003). Therefore, the center offers another workshop, *Writing Your Teaching Philosophy*, which is designed to introduce graduate students to the elements of a teaching philosophy statement as well as provide them with strategies for articulating their philosophy, regardless of their teaching experience. This workshop is framed around the important and elegantly simple work of Chism (1998) as well as that of O'Neal, Meizlish, and Kaplan (2007). In addition to these introductory workshops, the teaching consultants at our center are available for personal consultations on both teaching portfolios and teaching philosophy statements during which we are able to provide more targeted and discipline-specific feedback. These services are further supported through an extensive library of graduate student teaching portfolios, which graduate students are welcome to peruse on site, and through an additional workshop, the *Teaching Portfolio Review Panel*, in which experienced faculty members sit down with the TEACH Fellows and their portfolios so that they may provide them with additional feedback.

Evaluating Teaching Portfolios

Relatively little has been written about the teaching portfolio evaluation process in higher education, particularly regarding the graduate student teaching portfolio. A large portion of the literature, for instance, focuses on K-12 or pre-service teacher portfolios. Regarding higher education teaching portfolios, Centra (2000) delineates the variety of evaluation procedures followed at multiple institutions, concluding that, regardless of the evaluation process, such reports are expected to include an "array of instructional procedures, outcomes, and reflections that will give colleagues an opportunity to make valid decisions" (p. 93). In the most recent edition of *The Teaching Portfolio* (2010), one of the premier publications on teaching portfolios, Seldin and his co-authors offer a list of general items to consider in the evaluation of portfolios, such as alignment among the various elements (i.e., the teaching philosophy statement, sample syllabi, and classroom methodologies), efforts towards improved performance, and evidence of teaching effectiveness and student learning (pp. 44-45). One common refrain in the literature is the importance of reflection and commentary in teaching portfolios, not only for personal growth on the part of the portfolio creator, but also for ease of reading and understanding the contents of the portfolio (Centra, 2000; De Rijdt, Tiquet, Docy, & Devolder, 2006; Hurst, Wilson, & Cramer, 1998; Quinlan, 2002; Seldin, Miller, & Seldin, 2010; Wolf & Dietz, 1998). And as Wright, Knight, and Pomerleau (1999) assert, teaching portfolios "are documented self-evaluation exercises. This is significant because skill at self-evaluation in the form of reflection is desirable among academic staff/faculty" (p. 90). As such, throughout the development of the teaching portfolio, we constantly emphasize the significance of reflection and individualization as essential components of the portfolio and professional development in general.

Our evaluation criteria for graduate student teaching portfolios take into account many of the elements suggested in the literature. However, while much of the literature concentrates on the evaluation of the teaching methods described within a portfolio, our evaluation process emphasizes the successful communication of those methods. In other words, when evaluating the portfolios, we are not offering judgment or feedback on whether we agree with the creators' teaching decisions, but rather on how clearly they present the philosophy, artifacts, and context of their teaching. We urge Fellows to seek input regarding discipline-specific teaching pedagogy from faculty members or colleagues within their department. In doing so, it is our hope that their portfolios will serve them well in the future for purposes such as the job search, tenure and promotion, or award applications by providing others with a rich, reader-friendly look at their teaching.

One of the sticking points of many generalized teaching awards is the lack of an objective measure or specific criteria (Chism, 2006; Menges, 1996). However, we employ a standardized metric in evaluating our graduate students' portfolios that measures the effectiveness of professional appearance, organization, teaching philosophy statement, reflection, evidence of evaluation, and appendices on a five point scale (see Appendix A). Because an increasing number of hiring committees are requiring teaching philosophy statements from job applicants (Montell, 2003), with or without portfolios, we make it a required element for our program Fellows and give special attention to the document within our rubric. We also provide the Fellows with thorough, detailed feedback (typically three to six pages in length) relevant to each rubric category, highlighting the successes of the portfolio and making suggestions for improvement, specifically from the perspective of a hiring committee. Each of our experienced program consultants evaluates a portion of the portfolios so that we can provide the Fellows with timely and extensive feedback, and our team meets to compare notes on our evaluations of the portfolios as a whole to ensure that we are all in agreement on scores.

The process of selecting portfolios for recognition has evolved over the course of six years. Initially, we would select a small number of "finalists" from the group based on the rubric scores they received from TEACH Program staff members, and a committee of three faculty members would donate their time to meet and select the "winners" (typically first, second, and third place, followed by one or two honorable mentions). However, it became difficult to recruit busy faculty members who could find a common meeting time and evaluate five or more portfolios. That selection process eventually evolved into first asking faculty members to score the portfolios individually using the same rubric and adding up the scores to determine ranked "winners," then to simply giving unranked recognition to those Fellows who received the highest rubric scores from the staff evaluations. Each selection process we have utilized, from the most complicated to the simplest, has served our purposes because we are working with a small, self-contained group of students and a relatively minor, low-stakes award, and the initial evaluations are conducted by staff members who have broad knowledge of teaching portfolios.

Why Teaching Portfolio Awards?

Over the past few decades, the designation of teaching awards has become standard practice at institutions of higher education. The literature on teaching awards agrees that the majority of teaching awards are generally intended to demonstrate support for teaching and promote teaching excellence (Carusetta, 2001; Chism & Szabó, 1997; Chism, 2006; Dinham & Scott, 2002; Menges, 1996), and acknowledges that the criteria for granting teaching awards is often vague and, when articulated, varies greatly from award to award (Carusetta, 2001; Chism, 2006; Menges, 1996). Of those institutions or programs that do outline criteria to demonstrate teaching excellence, many utilize teaching portfolios as a method of documentation (Carusetta, 2001; Lunde & Barrett, 1996; Richlin & Manning, 1996). The literature also reveals that while some faculty resent the amount of time needed to compile the documentation required for award applications (Menges, 1996; Richlin & Manning, 1996), others appreciate and benefit from the reflection that results from the process of documenting achievements and teaching development (Dinham & Scott, 2002; Menges, 1996; Richlin & Manning, 1996). However, one thing the literature on teaching awards does not address is the value of rewarding outstanding teaching portfolios on their own merits.

Our decision to acknowledge a select group of outstanding portfolios completed by our Fellows each year was initially born out of an influx of scholarship funds donated by a textbook publishing company, allowing us to give our graduate students a little extra money as well as praise for their excellent work. When those funds were no longer available, we decided to continue recognizing exceptional work because that recognition offers more than simply a cash award: it offers tangible career as well as developmental benefits. One subset of educational research focuses on self-efficacy toward teaching as a positive factor in teaching behaviors as well as student outcomes, motivation, and achievement (such as Anderson, Greene, & Loewen, 1988; Gibson & Dembo, 1984; Ross, 1992; Tschannen-Moran & Hoy, 2001), some with particular regard to the self-efficacy of novice or graduate student instructors (Bray & Howard, 1980; Preito & Altmaier, 1994; Tschannen-Moran & Hoy, 2007). This literature points to the significant role of self-efficacy, or confidence, for instructors of all kinds, but especially less-experienced graduate student instructors. It is therefore important to note what might otherwise seem insignificant: the confidence granted by the simplest of awards.

Method

To determine the ways in which portfolio award recipients responded to their portfolio and award experience, as well as any benefits and drawbacks, interviews were conducted with six past award recipients. In this case study, each recipient was asked the same two questions: *What were the benefits (if any) of creating a teaching portfolio?* and *How did receiving recognition for your portfolio benefit you, if at all?* Interviewees were identified based upon their recognition as a teaching portfolio award winner and were contacted via email by the research team. In the email, the researchers indicated that information was being collected for a study, that the recipients' participation was optional, and that their responses would be kept anonymous. The interviewees represent a variety of disciplines, a range of teaching experiences, and are now at different places in their career paths (see Table 1).

Conceptual content analysis was conducted of the interview transcripts, with each author coding the transcripts independently to ensure interrater reliability. The transcripts were coded using an inductive grounded theory approach, allowing the dominant categories to emerge from the texts. This analysis yielded five salient categories related to the portfolio creation process and the experience of receiving an award for one's portfolio, with the two most prominent categories being the experience of gaining confidence and validation, and assistance with the job search process (see Table 2).

Results and Discussion

Graduate student Fellows in this case study who received acknowledgment for their teaching portfolios commented that, above all else, they gained confidence in their teaching as well as in the value of their documents. They also indicated that as a result of the confidence they felt about their portfolios, their job search process benefited. One former Fellow from Psychology, still completing her doctoral work, noted that receiving recognition for her portfolio "validated that [she was] going in the right direction," and encouraged her to show her portfolio to her colleagues and peers (personal interview, January 17, 2012). She also commented that she feels confident in updating her portfolio and using it on the job market, and has even already been able to use it for other award applications (personal interview, January 17, 2012). Another former award-winning Fellow from the field of Accounting, who has been working successfully in his first faculty position for over three years, stated that even when his colleagues urged him to waste no effort on the creation of his portfolio and advised him that many institutions would pay it little attention, receiving

Table 1. Interviewee Demographics

Discipline	Gender	Teaching experience	Where they were at the time of the award	Where they are now
Marriage and Family Therapy	Male	Experienced teacher	Final year of PhD program	Tenure-track faculty
Psychology	Female	Experienced teacher	2nd year of PhD program	Graduate student
Personal Financial Planning	Male	New teacher	2nd year of PhD program	Professional internship
Theater	Female	Experienced teacher	3rd year of PhD program	Tenure-track faculty
Nutrition	Female	New teacher	3rd year of PhD program	Tenure-track faculty
Accounting	Male	Experienced teacher	3rd year of PhD program	Tenure-track faculty

Table 2. Predominant Categories in Student Interview Commentary

Category	Response Rate (N= 6)
Gaining confidence or validation	100% (N = 6)
Assistance with job search	83.3 (N = 5)
Engaging in reflection	66.7 (N = 4)
Clarifying beliefs	50 (N = 3)
Line on CV	16.7 (N = 1)

recognition for his work instilled "greater confidence [in him] that [he] had a quality document that could be provided to potential employers" (personal interview, January 10, 2012). He added, "Had my portfolio not received recognition, and if the feedback I had received was mostly negative, I likely would not have felt comfortable distributing the portfolio to potential employers," continuing that his current institution did in fact read his portfolio in detail and considered it in their evaluation of him for the position (personal interview, January 10, 2012). Another former Fellow from the department of Theater, completing her first year as a faculty member, confirmed the same sentiment, revealing that receiving recognition for her portfolio did indeed give her "confidence in the work [she] had done"; she thus brought multiple copies of the document on her only job interview, impressing the committee that ultimately hired her (personal interview, January 13, 2012). One Marriage and Family Therapy Fellow, in the third year of his first faculty position, likewise agreed, asserting that his portfolio gave him confidence "that the product was good and that it was something [he] could stand behind. Any bit of confidence is helpful in the stressful job hunt" (personal interview, January 26, 2012).

These Fellows also revealed that by giving value to the hard work of creating a teaching portfolio, they gained confidence in their teaching itself and benefited overall from the reflective process. For instance, the graduate student from Psychology commented:

> Simply creating the portfolio (seeing all my students' evaluations in one place, constructing my improvement as an instructor over time, etc.) made me feel really good as an instructor. It gave me a boost of confidence by noticing how much I had improved over time and by noticing how much my students liked me. Receiving recognition for my portfolio just confirmed that others generally think I do a nice job teaching and do good work. (personal interview, January 17, 2012)

The Accounting Fellow acknowledged that through the documentation and reflection process, he was "forced to think more explicitly about the teaching methods [he] was using and the reasons why [he] was using such methods"; this process, he added, also helped him articulate himself during job interviews (personal interview, January 10, 2012). A former Fellow from the field of Nutrition, just beginning her first faculty position, also related that creating the portfolio was the first time she had ever considered her teaching philosophy or reflected on her syllabus. "This part of the portfolio," she noted, "helped [her] by making [her] take a step back" and asking her to look at her teaching "in a new light" (personal interview, January 21, 2012). She also confirmed, "Receiving recognition helped validate the effort I put forth on the portfolio. It was an encouragement and helped give me confidence in my work" (personal interview, January 21, 2012). The Marriage and Family Therapy Fellow also showed appreciation for reflective process, stating, "Compiling the portfolio gave me the tools I needed to talk about how I would be as a teacher and why I was a good fit" (personal interview, January 26, 2012). Finally, a former TEACH Fellow from the department of Personal Financial Planning, currently seeking his first faculty position, confirmed this notion of teaching confidence, adding: "Because I completed the portfolio after only my first semester teaching, it was a HUGE confidence boost for me when I received recognition…It made me realize that I can succeed at teaching. I have a desire to improve, and I felt validated that my desire was recognized" (personal interview, January 21, 2012).

Just as the literature confirms the importance of reflection in teaching portfolios, it also confirms the importance of reflection in effective teaching in general (Giovannelli, 2003). The very act of creating a portfolio should inspire reflection, as Wolf and Dietz (1998) write, "alone and in the company of others, in writing and in conversation, in planning and in documenting one's teaching" (p.12). That process of reflection and the promotion of deeper thinking about teaching can in fact help teachers to become more self-confident about their teaching practices, "which will influence their classroom practices in various ways," according to Tigelaar, et al. (2005, p. 604). Dinham and Scott (2002) likewise advocate the importance of the developmental teaching portfolio for young teachers, and assert that teachers struggle to reflect in the midst of daily tasks and teaching duties but need an opportunity to reflect on the big picture view, their accomplishments, and growth in the process. The Fellow from Personal Financial Planning, for instance, asserted that his portfolio "served as a guide throughout [his] other teaching experiences," influencing him to engage in "reflection-on-action" and that "reflection on [his] efforts in teaching… also helped [him] feel more confident as a teacher" (personal interview, January 21, 2012).

As the testimonials from our Fellows illustrate, the benefits of creating a teaching portfolio are significant. Likewise, there is considerable value in having one's portfolio reviewed with careful feedback, and recognition for a thoughtfully prepared document. Their comments bear a common thread in that they felt validated as teachers through the evaluation and award process. Whether we encourage a Fellow not to lose his passion for teaching, help to refine an explanation of why a particular method is used, or give someone the courage to take a portfolio forward in the job search (perhaps in a field or to an institution seemingly unfamiliar with portfolios), the evaluation process and the award are meaningful.

Limitations and Adaptations for Other Contexts

An obvious limitation of this work is the size of the sample; however, this limited group of Fellows still provided rich and, up to now, relatively rare insight from the student voice as to the benefit of portfolios, the feedback gained through the review process, and the resulting confidence and its perceived effect on teaching. However, the Fellows may represent a group of graduate students and future faculty members who are already well on their way to becoming excellent teachers; after all, they have taken time away from their graduate studies to participate in a teaching fellowship. This bias could be considered in future adaptations of the portfolio and review process with broader groups of graduate students. For example, on our campus, a teaching pedagogy class within the School of Business as well as the graduate program in Marriage and Family Therapy now require their students to complete teaching portfolios. Evaluating how these students perceive benefit from this component or how they might respond to the addition of an award component is one potential area for future study. Graduate schools and student organizations might also consider sponsoring teaching portfolio resources, training, and awards as a way of recognizing the significance of time invested in a commitment to thoughtful teaching and career. As seen in Appendix A, award committees or departments could use the attached rubric as a simple method of evaluation.

Conclusion

Although little has been written about teaching portfolio awards, there are numerous awards recognizing excellence in teaching. It seems that this award, in a roundabout way, also recognizes excellence in teaching by singling out the teaching portfolio as a product of teaching and reflection. Ultimately, our experience and the feedback of our Fellows communicates that there is a trickle-down structure to the benefits of our portfolio award system, beginning with the most practical and tangible (confidence building and career and professional enhancement) but also extending to the developmental (becoming more reflective practitioners). By giving value to teaching portfolios through an award system, an institution can encourage its graduate student instructors to engage in the reflective process, and therefore even those students who do not receive official recognition can reap the rewards of the portfolio creation experience.

Certainly this award is important because of the evaluation process and the work put into portfolio development on the part of the writer (the Fellow) and the evaluator (the consultant). In our experience, it is worth it. In the simplest terms, the award builds confidence in their teaching and gives value to the process of reflection, and reflection inspires better teaching. As such, this small act of showing appreciation for young graduate student instructors' work can have lasting impact on who they become as teachers.

References

Anderson, R.N., Greene, M.L., & Loewen, P.S. (1988). Relationships among teachers' and students' thinking skills, sense of efficacy, and student achievement. *The Alberta Journal of Educational Research 34,* 148–165.

Bray, J., & Howard, G. (1980). Methodological considerations in the evaluation of a teacher-training program. *Journal of Educational Psychology, 71*(1), 62–70.

Carusetta, E. (2001). Evaluating teaching through teaching awards. *New Directions for Teaching and Learning 88,* 31–40.

Centra, J.A. (2000). Evaluating the teaching portfolio: A role for colleagues. *New Directions for Teaching and Learning, 83,* 87–93.

Chism, N., & Szabó, B.L. (1997). Teaching awards: The problem of assessing their impact. In D. DeZure (Ed.), *To Improve the Academy 16,* 181–200.

Chism, N. (1998). Developing a philosophy of teaching statement." *Class Action, 1*(8).

Chism, N. (2006). Teaching awards: What do they award? *The Journal of Higher Education 77*(4), 589-617.

Clark, D., & Redmond, M. (1982). Small group instructional diagnosis: Final report (ERIC Document Reproduction Service, No. ED 217954) Seattle, WA: Washington University Department of Biology Education.

De Rijdt, C., Tiquet, E., Dochy, F., & Devolder, M. (2006). Teaching portfolios in higher education and their effects: An explorative study. *Teaching and Teacher Education, 22,* 1084–1093.

Dinham, S., & Scott, C. (2002). Awards for teaching excellence: Intentions and realities. AARE 2002 Conference Papers: Conference of the Australian Association for Research in Education. Retrieved from http://works.bepress.com/stephen_dinham/37/

Gibson, S., & Dembo, M.H. (1984). Teacher efficacy: A construct validation. *Journal of Educational Psychology, 76*(4), 569–582.

Giovanelli, M. (2003). Relationship between reflective disposition toward teaching and effective teaching. *The Journal of Educational Research, 96*(5), 293–309.

Hurst, B., Wilson, C., & Cramer, G. (1998). Professional teaching portfolios. *Phi Delta Kappan, 79*(8), pp. 578–582.

Lunde, J. P., & Barrett, L. A. (1996). Decentralized/Departmental reward systems. *New Directions for Teaching and Learning, 65,* 93–98.

Menges, R. (1996). Awards to individuals. *New Directions for Teaching and Learning, 65,* 3–9.

Montell, G. (2003, March 27). What's your philosophy on teaching, and does it matter? *The Chronicle of Higher Education.*

Murray, J. (1994) Why teaching portfolios? *Community College Review, 22*(1), 33–43.

O'Neal, C., Meizlish, D., & Kaplan, M. (2007). Writing a statement of teaching philosophy for the academic job search. *CRLT Occasional Paper* 23.

Preparing future faculty. (n.d.) Retrieved from http://www.preparing-faculty.org/

Prieto, L. R., & Altmaier, E. M. (1994). The relationship of prior training and previous teaching experience to self-efficacy among graduate teaching assistants. *Research in Higher Education, 35*(4), 481–497.

Quinlan, K. M. (2002). Inside the peer review process: How academics review a colleague's teaching portfolio. *Teaching and Teacher Education, 18*, 1035–1049.

Richlin, L., & Manning, B. (1996). Using portfolios to document teaching excellence. *New Directions for Teaching and Learning, 65*, 65–70.

Ross, J. A. (1992). Teacher efficacy and the effects of coaching on student achievement. *Canadian Journal of Education, 17*, 51–65.

Seldin, P. (2004). *The teaching portfolio: A practical guide to improved performance and promotion/tenure decisions.* 3rd Edition. Bolton, MA: Anker.

Seldin, P., Miller, J. E., & Seldin, C. (2010). *The teaching portfolio: A practical guide to improved performance and promotion/tenure decisions.* 4th ed. San Francisco, CA: Jossey-Bass.

Sorcinelli, M.D., & Davis, B. G. (1996). Honoring exemplary teachers in research universities. *New Directions for Teaching and Learning, 65*, 3–9.

Tigelaar, D., Dolmans, D., Wolfhagen, I., & van der Vietuen, C. (2005). Quality issues in judging portfolios: Implications for organizing teaching portfolio assessment procedures. *Studies in Higher Education 30*(5), 595–610.

Tschannen-Moran, M. & Hoy, A.W. (2001). Teacher efficacy: Capturing an elusive construct. *Teaching and Teacher Education, 17*, 793–805.

Tschannen-Moran, M. & Hoy, A.W. (2007). The differential antecedents of self-efficacy beliefs of novice and experienced teachers. *Teaching and Teacher Education, 23*, 944–956.

Wolf, K., & Dietz, M. (1998). Teaching portfolios: Purposes and possibilities. *Teacher Education Quarterly, 25*, 9–22.

Wright, W.A., Knight, P.T., & Pomerleau, N. (1999). Portfolio people: Teaching and learning dossiers and innovation in higher education. *Innovative Higher Education, 24*(2), 89–103.

Allison Boye is an assistant director at Texas Tech University's Teaching, Learning, and Professional Development Center, where she works with faculty as well as directs their graduate student development program, the TEACH Program. She currently sits on the conference committee for the Professional and Organizational Development Network in Higher Education (POD), and has also served as chair for the POD Innovation Award and on the Executive Council for the Texas Faculty Developers Network. She has most recently published research on the topics of consultation practices, peer observation, and graduate student development.

Suzanne Tapp is the Director of the Teaching, Learning, and Professional Development Center at Texas Tech University. She is a member of the Core Committee of the Professional and Organizational Development Network in Higher Education (POD) and serves on the editorial board of the *Journal of Student Learning through Mentored Scholarship*. Her research interests include social media in the classroom, graduate student development, and faculty consultation practices.

Micah Meixner Logan is an assistant director at Texas Tech University's Teaching, Learning and Professional Development Center (TLPDC). Through her role at the TLPDC, she works with advisors, graduate students, and faculty to support the advancement of undergraduate education. Her research interests include service learning, graduate student development, and reflective teaching.

Appendix A
Teaching Portfolio Rubric

Detailed Ratings:	Poor	Fair	Good	Very Good	Excellent
Professional Appearance Are the font sizes, colorings, spacing, etc. consistent and do they aid the reader in processing the information? Is the portfolio free of grammatical and spelling errors? Is the portfolio polished and ready for a job interview?	1	2	3	4	5
Organization Is the portfolio easily navigated? Do the sections have a logical flow? Does the reviewer have to search for content?	1	2	3	4	5
Teaching Philosophy Statement Is the teaching statement well-articulated? Is there evidence of the philosophy found throughout the portfolio? Did the philosophy give a "picture" of what the instructor is like in the classroom?	1	2	3	4	5
Evidence of Evaluation Does the instructor use classroom assessment techniques? Did the instructor seek feedback from others (students, peers, faculty members) about his/her teaching? Is there evidence of willingness to change based on feedback from others?	1	2	3	4	5
Reflection Were reflective statements used throughout the document to make it self-explanatory? Are reflective statements used to give the reviewer insight into "why they do what they do"? Is the portfolio thoughtful and thorough, without being overwhelming?	1	2	3	4	5
Appendices Is all of the material in the appendix referred to in the body of the portfolio? Is there material included in the appendices that seems irrelevant or like overkill? Are summary tables used when necessary (e.g. evaluations) to condense the size of the appendices?	1	2	3	4	5

Overall Rating of the Portfolio: 1 - Unacceptable; 2 - Needs more work and time; 3 - Good starting point; 4 - Strong; 5 - Excellent

Chapter 6
Using Collaborative Inquiry to Investigate Reflective Teaching Portfolios as Award Criteria

Kim West, Leah Ferguson, Allison Henderson, Chantal Kawalilak, Colleen Krushelinski, Emily Morris, Catherine Neumann, & Serene Smyth

Using collaborative inquiry, this chapter presents lessons learned in developing and using reflective teaching portfolios as the criteria for a graduate student teacher award at the University of Saskatchewan. We discuss ways to modify existing award criteria while providing recommendations that institutions developing similar criteria could consider.

From 2009 to 2011, a group of graduate student teachers and one educational developer met on several occasions to investigate the effectiveness of using reflective portfolios as the award criteria for the Provost's Outstanding Graduate Student Teacher Award at the University of Saskatchewan. This article describes a type of action-oriented research called collaborative inquiry upon which we modeled our investigations. First, using narrative, we describe the award and our experiences in applying for or adjudicating the award. Second, we discuss the benefits and limitations of using reflective teaching portfolios as award criteria while providing suggestions for modification of existing award criteria at the University of Saskatchewan. Third, we provide a general set of recommendations for other institutions to consider in developing criteria for similar graduate student teacher awards. Finally, we reflect on the broader implications of using collaborative inquiry in academia to empower graduate student voices and drive social change, while strengthening and/or building community connections.

Collaborative Inquiry

Collaborative inquiry (also known as co-operative inquiry) is a type of action-oriented research in which co-inquirers or collaborators explore an issue that is meaningful to them, and in so doing, learn from each other (Heron & Reason, 2001; Reason, 1999). For this reason, collaborative inquiry is often described as "doing research *with* other people, not *on* them" (Barrett, 2002; p. 281; Heron & Reason, 2001; Reason, 1999; Reason & Heron, 1986). During the process, co-inquirers work together to determine a central problem or question that will be the eventual focus of the inquiry, and later on, contribute to the design and management of all aspects of the study, including the conclusions drawn (Reason, 1999). At the same time, collaborators fully participate in the research by inquiring into the nature of the problem or question and by undertaking some type of action (Park, 2001; Reason, 1999).

Collaborative inquiry, like other types of action-oriented research, is strategic in that it focuses on transforming some aspect of practice in the real world (Mitchell-Williams, et al., 2004). It is participatory (and in some cases, emancipatory) in that non-experts, rather than experts, play the lead role in developing ideas, working together to challenge their perceptions and transform practice (Barrett, 2002; Park, 2001; Reason, 1999). Collaborative inquiry is democratic in that all decisions are made collaboratively. Rapport building is thus an integral part of the research process and may be facilitated through a focus on dialogue (Mitchell-Williams, et al., 2004). Finally, collaborative inquiry is distinctive from other social research methods because it emphasizes learning and the construction of shared meaning (Mitchell-Williams, et al., 2004). This challenges conventional Western research epistemologies (Park, 2001; Ospina, El Hadidy & Hofmann-Pinilla, 2008) and in so doing, helps to transform academic perspectives of what should count as research (Eisner, 1997).

Methodology

Our study follows the methodology of collaborative inquiry as set forth by Heron and Reason (2001), based upon the earlier work of Reason and Heron (1986). The process of collaborative inquiry is systematic, with cycles of critical reflection and action that in turn examine experience and practice, differentiating the research process from uncritical subjectivity (Reason, 1999).

Writing narratives of our experiences applying for the award and later sharing them with each other was the first cornerstone of our process. Using narrative inquiry helped us to construct a deeper understanding of ourselves and of the academic culture around us (Connelly & Clandinin, 2006). We found the process of creating a narrative and reading the narratives of others personally and professionally encouraging. Sharing our experiences with each other helped us to bond early on in the process and, as a result, to discover and disclose more readily about ourselves, which led to greater rapport and empathy amongst the collaborators in our group (Mitchell-Williams, et al., 2004).

Dialogue was the second cornerstone of our process because of the role it played in prompting us to think about and act upon changes in our professional practice. This was significant for three reasons. First, our narratives were written primarily from our reflections on experience. Second, dialogue fostered critical reflection which involved asking each other questions about our experiences and actions and, in turn, thinking critically and systematically about our perceptions or intentions. This critical reflection led to the personal growth and transformation that we all experienced as one of the primary benefits of the study (Mitchell-Williams, et al., 2004). Third, through dialogue we gained new perspectives beyond our own experiences leading to a shared understanding that informed the suggestions and recommendations that we have made in this study.

Narratives

The following narratives describe the criteria for the Provost's Outstanding Graduate Student Teacher Award, our individual experiences in developing and using reflective teaching portfolios and, for one of us, in serving as a peer reviewer on the award selection committee. We hope that our narratives will be reassuring to other new teachers who are facing similar anxieties about teaching or documenting their teaching practice. Each narrative is unique in that it illustrates different successes and challenges that could be associated with developing, using and/or adjudicating reflective teaching portfolios before, after, and/or during an award process.

Using Reflective Portfolios as the Basis of the Award

Kim's story (Educational Developer, The Gwenna Moss Centre for Teaching Effectiveness)

In 2009, I was asked to sit on the committee responsible for drafting the criteria for the new Provost's Outstanding Graduate Student Teacher Award. This award was one of several newly developed awards at the University of Saskatchewan with the purpose of recognizing and rewarding excellence in teaching. In addition to the award for graduate student teachers, there was an award for new faculty, College-level awards for faculty, and several awards to recognize excellence in areas of institutional priority, including Aboriginal education, international teaching, innovation in learning, and graduate teaching.

The purpose of the Outstanding Graduate Student Teacher Award was to recognize and reward graduate students who had demonstrated outstanding promise as teachers and taught for at least one academic term. At the University of Saskatchewan, graduate students are involved in a variety of roles from teaching assistant to marker. In some cases, they may even be an instructor with the sole responsibility for a course. As a result, we wanted our award criteria to be flexible enough to encourage graduate students with diverse roles and responsibilities to apply for the award.

The teaching portfolio, initially developed to diversify the ways that faculty could describe and document their teaching (Knapper, 1995; Knapper & Wright, 2001), appeared to be well suited to our needs. In addition, the criteria for other teaching awards in Canada (e.g., 3M National Teaching Fellowship) already closely followed the model of the teaching portfolio. We expected that in some departments, graduate students would be given more opportunity to teach than in others. As a result, to emphasize both practice and teaching development (Plaza, et al., 2007) we decided to base the criteria for our award on the model of a reflective teaching portfolio, similar to the models described by Millis (1995), Hutchings (1998), and Border (2002), which include some evidence of effective teaching in combination with reflective components.

The reflective teaching portfolio was limited to 15 pages, including a nomination letter, teaching philosophy statement, description of teaching responsibilities, student or peer evaluation results (including the candidate's response to the feedback), and supporting materials which could include the description of an innovative teaching strategy, reflection-on-practice, and ongoing professional development. We provided numerous resources for graduate students to learn about developing reflective portfolios: non-credit courses offered each year through the College of Graduate Studies & Research, a short course on the teaching portfolio (eight to ten weeks in length), one-on-one portfolio consultations (offered anytime), a collection of model portfolios, and a popular teaching portfolio website (http://www.usask.ca/gmcte/resources/portfolio). When the award had been in place for a few years, I started to notice the majority of applicants were graduate students from the non-credit or short courses that we offered. I began to wonder what we could do differently to modify the criteria to better suit the needs of all graduate student teachers across campus. To seek out an answer to this question, I sought the help of the graduate student teachers who had previously applied for the award.

Self-Reflection in the Teaching Portfolio: A Tool for Change

Allison's story (PhD Candidate, School of Environment & Sustainability)

I am new to teaching as a primary instructor. I recently created my reflective teaching portfolio for the graduate teaching award based on my work in developing and teaching an upper-level ecology course. Even though I had previously learned how to build a portfolio prior to the nomination (as part of one of our non-credit graduate courses), I found formalizing my reflective teaching practice a surprisingly difficult, yet worthwhile, task.

For me, preparing a reflective portfolio involved a real and repeated commitment to professional as well as personal reflection. Self-reflection, or the setting aside of time to reflect on the consistency of personal and professional values and actions, is not something that budding natural scientists are typically taught how to do, which is why, perhaps, every rigorous and objective bone in my body initially pushed back. It took a leap outside my comfort zone and a renewed dedication to reflective practice to create an authentic portfolio that represents who I am as a teacher today. The impetus of preparing a competitive portfolio for the award helped me to take this leap. I learned how to use reflective writing throughout the portfolio, and ample evidence from peer and student feedback, to draw out the themes that underlie my approach to teaching. In surpassing these limits, I gained valuable new skills in reflective practice and creative writing and, in effect, created a transformative tool that I can revisit over the course of my career.

How will my teaching portfolio serve as a tool to transform my teaching? It captured and demonstrated my core teaching values and beliefs early on in my career, which act later on as a benchmark for my growth as a teacher. I plan to return to my teaching portfolio after every teaching experience to reflect, compare, and adjust…ultimately mapping my evolution as a teacher over time. This process of self-awareness helps to transform my teaching over time by pushing me beyond my perceived boundaries and making my reflective practice tangible. Preparing this teaching portfolio was, while difficult, undeniably worthwhile.

The Teaching Portfolio: A Worthy Adversary

Chantal's story (PhD student, College of Kinesiology)

The teaching portfolio serves as an objective tool for the reflection and development of one's teaching method, in the monitoring of one's personal development as an instructor, and last, but certainly not least, as a comparative device amongst potential candidates for teaching awards and promotions. A tool used for so many areas of measure should be straightforward and relatively easy to compile. In fact, the creation of a teaching portfolio is neither of these things, especially when the available courses on the topic are out of reach.

Even in a college that values teaching, I find myself under the advisement of a committee that does not share my values in teaching development. I have completed my Master's and am in the process of working on my PhD within the same college. During both degrees, I requested to take part in one of the graduate courses our university offers with a focus on teaching portfolios. Each time my committee overruled my request in favour of more scientific and research savvy courses. However, as part of my scholarship, I am required to teach. When nominated for the graduate teaching award, I found myself spending numerous hours researching portfolio contents and requirements, creating and recreating components, and essentially getting behind in every aspect of my research and course work because I was unable to attend one of these courses.

In the world of academia, time is a valuable entity of which I have little. The time spent on the creation of the teaching portfolio could have been better spent on further developing my teaching skills, researching current topics and issues, improving lectures and labs for my students, or further developing my content and/or teaching-related knowledge. Instead, the creation of this multifactorial tool was at the foremost of the queue in my frontal cortex. I do not believe that such a high weighting should be placed on the teaching portfolio at a graduate student level; doing so will merely add to the pile of requirements and time commitments that a graduate student already has.

However, it has been said that anything worth doing takes time; I now fully understand this statement. The teaching portfolio is an objective measure and monitor of teaching effectiveness and a reflective means for development—a tool that is often times difficult to obtain, especially in areas of awards and promotions. In conclusion, I find myself torn. I started out as the 'devil's advocate' and now I find myself attracted to this tool, which I was previously so fond of calling my nemesis.

A Bittersweet Journey

Leah's story (PhD Candidate, College of Kinesiology)

I recently applied for the graduate teaching award, and found it to be a more challenging process then initially anticipated. In fact, reflecting on and documenting my commitment to teaching and learning was somewhat bittersweet. On one hand, going through the application process instilled me with a sense of accomplishment and pride as a graduate student teacher. It was also satisfying to be able to create a teaching portfolio that would express my dedication to teaching and learning. On the other hand, looking at my "completed" teaching portfolio almost made me feel pressured to do more and strive higher.

Reflecting on one area in particular—my continued involvement in professional development activities—left me feeling perhaps the most tense, almost as if I was worried that what I am currently doing is not enough. I think part of this pressure stemmed from being a graduate student teacher and never fully feeling one hundred percent confident or competent as a teacher. Even after attending and participating in a variety of professional development workshops, courses, and events, I cannot help but think there must be more that I can do to develop, grow, and flourish as a teacher.

Although developing a teaching portfolio was challenging at times, I certainly had not expected to feel tense and unsure of myself from engaging in this process. That being said, creating the portfolio was, without a doubt, incredibly rewarding. The pressure that I initially felt evolved into a healthy form of intrinsic motivation to continue to improve as a teacher, and since, has served as a reminder that I will always be able to improve as a teacher regardless of my stage of career. In addition, I feel that this journey of reflecting on and documenting my commitment to teaching and learning will be beneficial in any future academic endeavors. In fact, after noticing the amount of time that I was putting into my teaching portfolio for the award application, my PhD supervisor commented that the process appeared to be just as intense as applying for tenure. At the end of the application process, I feel quite fortunate in having a teaching portfolio that I am able to return to at this stage of my career and use as a reflective tool to see how my teaching evolves over time.

Selecting the Award Winners

Colleen's story (Peer Reviewer, Selection Committee)

As a graduate student peer invited to sit on the 2011 Selection Committee I was grateful for the use of teaching portfolios as part of the application process. This was my first time serving on a selection committee and I was a bit overwhelmed while at the same time quite excited about the prospects of working with an awards committee. I was, however, not feeling very confident about my ability to be objective nor to be able to choose only one outstanding teacher amongst the many graduate students who had been nominated for the award. Thank goodness for the prerequisite of a teaching portfolio as part of the submission procedure for it provided me with well-defined criteria by which to assess nominees.

I think without such a document to compel nominees to think deeply about *how* and *why* they teach the way they do and articulate *who* they are as teachers and learners, I would have been utterly bewildered in the execution of the task at hand. Instead, reading through the portfolios genuinely inspired and moved me. The depth of reflection required to construct a teaching portfolio made the selection process a little less daunting in that it afforded me the opportunity to embark on a personal and professional journey for each of the applicants. For example, the portfolios were helpful in constructing an authentic picture of the applicants, for instance who they were and what they believed or valued about effective teaching and learning. The strongest portfolios were ones in which nominees connected their philosophy, beliefs, values or strategies to feedback from peers and students, and in so doing, demonstrated their dedication to teaching, refining their teaching practice, and listening to their students. Thus, I was not only able to glimpse into the 'hearts and minds' of each of the graduate teachers but was able to hear another important voice: the voices of students. Ultimately, it was the testimony of the students that distinguished the award-winning applicant from the others. Being a part of this process required me to ruminate about the role of teaching and learning at the university and, in doing so, it expanded my awareness of the importance of a reflective teaching practice, as well as the significance of teaching awards in enhancing the value of teaching and learning at a research-intensive university.

From the Reflective to Professional: The Award Process as Stepping Stone

Emily's story (PhD Candidate, Department of English)

When I was nominated for the graduate teaching award, I had already created a reflective teaching portfolio as part of one of our graduate teaching courses. This had been my first experience with creating a teaching portfolio, and I thought of it as a good way to collect together the evidence I had of effective teaching from my practice.

I enjoyed creating materials for my reflective portfolio, including a teaching metaphor and philosophy statement, and felt they were of great personal benefit to me as a teacher, but I did not see them as being relevant to any professional evaluation of my teaching. I expected I would excise these components entirely when updating my portfolio for the graduate teaching award. In order to meet the stricter requirements of the award application, I culled materials from my original reflective portfolio and tightened up connections between evidence from my teaching practice and statements made throughout the portfolio. The criteria for the award portfolio specifically requested a teaching philosophy statement and reflective commentary, as did the guidelines for my original portfolio. Since the stakes were higher for the award ($2000 is a pretty substantial sum to a poor graduate student), however, I worked harder at proving that my philosophy and practice matched up. I was surprised to find that what I had considered to be personal and not useful in a professional capacity was easily honed into a more professional shape simply through a more structured use of language and organization.

I came out of the nomination process with a concise and rigorous portfolio, and a new understanding that reflection could be part of professional evidence, rather than simply a tool for personal improvement. In portfolios, and even cover letters for the job applications I have since been tackling, I am able to confidently draw connections between my teaching experiences, reflections, and evidence that I have collected from my teaching practice. The award application for me served not only as an impetus to refine the materials and connections in my original portfolio, but also to reinforce, in a practical way, the concept that reflection is a valuable professional tool.

The Portfolio as Continued Personal and Professional Development

Catherine's story (PhD Candidate, College of Education)

Twelve years ago, with my Bachelor of Education in one hand, and my teaching portfolio in the other, I got my first teaching job. For the last twelve years, I have been an elementary school teacher. During those twelve years my passion for teaching grew, my care for the students grew, and my abilities as a teacher grew and, from this, I realized that I wanted to make a larger impact on education. I went back to university to obtain a PhD so that I could teach teachers about teaching.

I was concerned about my transition from elementary school to university, but this started to subside when I enrolled in one of the graduate teaching courses offered at the University of Saskatchewan, where I was first introduced to the reflective teaching portfolio. I began revising my portfolio from a scattered, amateur, and underdeveloped version and in so doing, began to see how I 'fit in' at the university. My confidence began to grow.

While developing my portfolio for the graduate teaching award, the scattered underdeveloped pieces came together and I gained a fuller foundational understanding of myself in my new role. Working through my teaching philosophy reaffirmed and renewed my commitment to reflective teaching practice. I improved my teaching through this process because it helped me to reflect, re-assess, and re-define my practice— leading to an alignment between my teaching philosophy, learning outcomes, lesson plans and strategies, and assessments.

The portfolio process helped me to continue my personal and professional development as a teacher and I now understand more fully the what, why, and how of my practice. My initial desire to make a larger impact and teach future teachers has become even stronger, because I now have a stronger, more defined, aligned and confident undergird to my practice, that I think shows in my university classrooms.

With My Portfolio in Hand: Transforming Institutional Culture

Serene's story (PhD Candidate, College of Kinesiology)

In the university setting we talk about culture a great deal. We talk of creating culture and of changing it. Lately, the institutional culture around teaching has been changing at our university. I think for a long time, many years before I got to graduate school, teaching was an afterthought for graduate students; it was likely an afterthought for most faculty too. But times are changing. I think our institution as a whole is now placing more focus on teaching and this is flowing down to the graduate level. Declines in enrollment, the devaluation of a degree, and an economic downturn means more seats are open in our classrooms. This is where effective teaching comes in; good teachers have full classrooms and satisfied students that go on to take other courses. Ultimately that is what we as teachers want and what the institution wants as well.

One of the ways our university is making teaching a priority is by rewarding excellence in this field. In 2010 I was nominated for the graduate teaching award. Getting all of the documentation ready for my portfolio was no easy feat. But in the end, I had a portfolio that was a wonderful blend of my reflections on teaching, evaluations from students and peers, along with evidence that I included to showcase my commitment to professional development in teaching. I think that the type and amount of documentation required in these portfolios plays a role in changing the culture of teaching on campus. More sophisticated portfolios elevate teaching and its evaluation to a higher level, which in turn means that teaching can be taken more seriously in academic rewards and hiring. I have seen this first hand.

My teaching portfolio played an important role in getting the job that I held between my Masters and Doctorates at the University of Saskatchewan. In the fall of 2010, I applied for a curriculum development position on campus. While I did not give the hiring committee my entire portfolio, I selected certain elements from my reflective portfolio that I felt best related to the position. After submitting my portfolio for the teaching award earlier that year I knew it like the back of my hand. When it came time for my big interview, I had tangible examples of my educational practices and I could answer the challenging questions about my beliefs and positions on education because I had already grappled with these questions while developing my portfolio. Despite the fact that my hands were shaking like a leaf under the table the interview went great and I got the job. In a later conversation with a member of the hiring committee, I discovered that my experience and dedication to teaching played an equal role to my research background in my hiring.

I am now back to being a full time student who teaches regularly on campus. My teaching philosophy statement continues to evolve as my experience in education increases. I am optimistic about applying for a faculty position in a few years. As institutions continue to invest in and value teaching, I know I will be well positioned with my teaching portfolio in hand.

Discussion

Benefits of Reflective Teaching Portfolios as Award Criteria

Despite the time and effort required, we all agreed that developing a reflective teaching portfolio was worthwhile. On a personal level, many of us realized that reflection helped us to transform our understanding of ourselves: who we are and how we teach. From the perspective of a peer reviewer, this was significant in portraying the unique abilities and strengths of individual applicants. In addition, the reflective format of a portfolio could be useful in showcasing voices and experiences beyond those of the applicant, including student voices.

In our professional practice, the portfolio was beneficial in several ways.

For those of us currently teaching, we discussed and/or tried new ways to use the portfolio as a tool to reflect on our teaching practice. This raised an important point in our discussions about how engaging in the reflective process can continually remind us of our teaching goals and strengths. We thought this might be important for teachers during times when confidence is particularly low, such as when a lecture is poorly received. Perhaps the most tangible benefit of having and using a portfolio is in getting a teaching position, which very fortunately happened for two of us. Another hidden benefit was that reflection helped us to feel more confident when expressing our thoughts and ideas about teaching and learning during the interview process.

Limitations of Reflective Teaching Portfolios as Award Criteria

Our stories also reveal some of the potential problems and limitations of using reflective teaching portfolios as criteria for graduate student teaching awards. Reflection, by its very nature, requires an extended time commitment. This in itself likely prevented many graduate students from applying for our award, especially those who faced challenges from academic committees or departments when requesting to spend time on teaching development activities. This could be one of several reasons why some of our students were less likely to take advantage of programs such as courses or workshops, which would have offered them a greater level of support when applying for the award. This could also be why graduate students who had spent time previously reflecting on their teaching practice (either as part of a course or by using our other resources) applied more often for the award.

Another limitation of using reflective portfolios in award criteria is related to using standard forms of evidence to demonstrate effective teaching. For example, the University of Saskatchewan uses a standardized course evaluation tool (i.e., Student Evaluation of Education Quality, SEEQ) for students to provide summative feedback on the instructor's teaching and on the quality of the course. However, the instrument often overlooks graduate student teachers, leaving them without critical feedback from their students. To address this in the future, we suggest a modification of the existing award criteria to provide a more general set of guidelines for graduate student teachers on collecting summative feedback as well as examples and guidelines for other types of feedback (e.g., formative) that could be included in the portfolio.

Guidelines/ Recommendations

The findings from this collaborative inquiry have provided insight thus far into how reflective teaching portfolios have contributed to the personal and professional development of graduate student teachers at the University of

Saskatchewan and the limitations that may arise when using portfolios in award criteria. Next, we provide a general set of recommendations that we hope will be useful for institutions that are developing criteria for similar teaching awards:

1. Graduate teaching awards need to be well-advertised to students when they begin their graduate work, so they are aware of the kinds of evidence they need to begin gathering from their teaching as well as the kinds of support and teaching development opportunities that are available to them. In addition, conversations about the award and its criteria should occur regularly across campus to reinforce the importance of balancing teaching with research responsibilities. Similarly, administrators, staff, or faculty responsible for developing award criteria should consult with academic units to develop a better understanding of the expectations and demands that are being placed on graduate students from supervisors, academic committees, departments, or funding agencies.
2. Resources, examples, workshops, and other supports for developing teaching portfolios should be widely available in numerous formats to accommodate a variety of needs. For example, in our study not all graduate students were supported in their desire to complete a workshop or course on developing a portfolio. Resources such as one-on-one consultations, videos, guides, or other online resources are necessary additions to complement workshops and courses because they are accessible at any time, and in particular, closer to application deadlines.
3. The criteria and the language of the criteria need to be very explicit. To this end, a rubric for evaluating portfolios might be developed and made available to applicants when they apply. We also recommend providing examples of model portfolios for graduate students to consult, both in-house and online.
4. The awards criteria should consider the extent to which graduate students will have access to required documentation from their teaching practice (e.g., SEEQ or other standardized evaluations). The ways in which standardized evaluations are administered in graduate-student taught classes across the university might also be investigated and recommendations made to appropriate parties, in view of how students might make use of the evaluations.

Overall, we suggest that institutions begin the process of developing award criteria by initiating conversations with graduate student teachers about their experiences, needs, and interests. Most importantly, administrators, staff, faculty and/or others responsible for developing teaching award criteria should consider the ways in which teaching is valued at their institution and whether students in different departments and disciplines have equal access to support and resources.

Benefits of Collaborative Inquiry

We feel that collaborative inquiry is an especially appropriate means by which to tackle topics in academia such as teaching awards that are of common interest to administrators, staff, faculty, and students. First, the nature of this study created a rare opportunity for academic staff and graduate student teachers to learn from each other. On a broader scale, inquiry could be useful for breaking down barriers in academia by fostering understanding and rapport amongst individuals of disparate groups. Some authors have already used collaborative inquiry as a means to build relationships amongst experts and non-experts across the academic-practitioner divide (Ospina, El-Hadidy, & Hofmann-Pinilla, 2008). Second, the process of collaborative inquiry is considerably more egalitarian and autonomous than typical social research methods involving consultations or focus groups with students. Collaborative inquiry involves active learning, and in so doing, empowers students to not only think about but to take action on a topic that matters to them. This in itself models for students how to engage in social action and/or change. A limitation of collaborative inquiry is the amount of time it requires. Students are busy individuals, and as a result the logistics of organizing and scheduling meetings was sometimes a challenge.

Conclusions

Our study analyzed the experiences of graduate student teachers and one educational developer at a specific institution. Further investigations at other institutions, involving other groups or stakeholders, would no doubt yield other helpful suggestions. In particular, we think it may have been useful to expand our study to include more academic staff representatives from the award selection committee and others who were involved in drafting the award criteria, as well as graduate students who had not already applied for the award. The insight garnered from these individuals would have provided different perspectives on how to better improve reflective teaching portfolios as criteria in the award process.

Despite the time and effort required, we all agreed that developing a reflective teaching portfolio as part of the award process was worthwhile. The limitations we faced as individuals and the recommendations we make in this article mainly concern improvements in communication, clarity, timing, and resource accessibility with respect to teaching award criteria, particularly for graduate students who come from academic cultures that do not place as much value on teaching development as others do.

References

Barrett, R. (2002). Mentor supervision and development- exploration of lived experience. *Career Development International, 7*(5), 279-283.

Border, L. L. B. (2002). The Socratic portfolio: A guide for future faculty. *PS Online, 25*(4), 739-743.

Connelly, F. M., & Clandinin, D.J. (2006). Narrative inquiry. In J.L.Green, G. Camilli, & P. Elmore (Eds.), *Handbook of complementary methods in education research* (pp.477-487). Mahwah, NJ: Lawrence Erlbaum.

Eisner, E. W. (1997). The promise and perils of alternative forms of data representation. *Educational Researcher, 26*(6), 4-10.

Heron, J., & Reason, P. (2001). The practice of co-operative inquiry: Research 'with' rather than 'on' people. In P. Reason & H. Bradbury (Eds.), *Handbook of action research* (pp.179-188). Thousand Oaks, CA: Sage.

Hutchings, P. (1998). Teaching portfolios as a tool for TA development. In M. Marinocovich, J. Prostko, & F. Stout (Eds.), *The professional development of graduate teaching assistants* (pp.235-248). Bolton, MA: Anker.

Knapper, C. (1995). The origin of teaching portfolios. *Journal on Excellence in College Teaching, 6*(1), 45-56.

Knapper, C., & Wright, W.A. (2001). Using portfolios to document good teaching: Premises, purposes, and practices. *New Directions for Teaching and Learning, 88*,19-29.

Millis, B. J. (1995). Shaping the reflective portfolio: A philosophical look at the mentoring role. *Journal on Excellence in College Teaching, 6*(1), 65-73.

Mitchell-Williams, Z., Wilkins, P., McLean, M., Nevin, W., Wastell, K., & Wheat, R. (2004). The importance of the personal element in collaborative research. *Educational Action Research, 12*(3), 329-346.

Ospina, S., El-Hadidy, W., & Hofmann-Pinilla, A. (2008). Cooperative inquiry for learning and connectedness. *Action Learning: Research and Practice, 5*(2), 131-147.

Park, P. (2001). Knowledge and participatory research. In P. Reason & H. Bradbury (Eds.), *Handbook of action research* (pp.81-90). Thousand Oaks, CA: Sage.

Plaza, C. M., Draugalis, J. R., Slack, M. K., Skrepnek, G. H., & Sauer, K. A. (2007). Use of reflective portfolios in Health Sciences education. *American Journal of Pharmaceutical Education, 71*(2), 34-40.

Reason, P. (1999). Integrating action and reflection through co-operative inquiry. *Management Learning, 30*, 207-226.

Reason, P., & Heron, J. (1986). Research with people: The paradigm of co-operative experiential inquiry. *Person Centred Review, 1*(4), 456-75.

Kim West is an Educational Development Specialist at The Gwenna Moss Centre for Teaching Effectiveness at the University of Saskatchewan who works with graduate student teachers, sessional lecturers, and faculty. She holds a PhD in Earth Sciences from Carleton University and is a Professional Affiliate with the Department of Geography & Planning at the University of Saskatchewan.

Leah Ferguson is a PhD Candidate and instructor in the College of Kinesiology at the University of Saskatchewan.

Allison Henderson is a PhD Candidate in the School of Environment and Sustainability. She studies social and ecological dimensions of prairie conservation and teaches a fourth-year grassland ecology class for the Department of Biology.

Chantal Kawalilak (M.Sc.) is currently a PhD Student in the College of Kinesiology at the University of Saskatchewan. Her main area of research is to determine the affect of impact and loading on the musculoskeletal system. As part of her PhD, she aims to investigate how physical activity affects the ultimate strength of bone, measured using an engineering based simulation model in combination with computer tomographic imaging of the upper and lower extremities.

Colleen Krushelinski holds a B.Ed., as well as a B.A. and M.A. in History from the University of Saskatchewan. After many years spent researching and teaching at the university, Colleen decided it was time for a change and will be re-locating to the Central Highlands of Mexico where she intends to explore the rich history, culture and traditions of the region.

Emily Morris holds a PhD in English Literature from the University of Saskatchewan and teaches at St. Thomas More College. Her research centers on Victorian author Elizabeth Gaskell.

Catherine Neumann was an elementary school teacher for ten years and a district teachers' coach for four years. She obtained her PhD in Education at the University of Saskatchewan and is now a sessional lecturer for the University of Manitoba and the University of Winnipeg.

Serene Smyth is a PhD Candidate in Kinesiology at the University of Saskatchewan. She conducts research with Aboriginal youth and looks at how physical activity affects learning and mental health.

Chapter 7
Identifying Excellent Teaching Through Graduate Student Teaching Award Nomination Portfolios

Stephanie V. Rohdieck, Dawn Walts, Lindsay Bernhagen, & Kathleen M. Hallihan

---

This chapter reports on a study of one university's selection committee for a graduate student teaching award. Although this committee evaluated teaching portfolios based on established criteria, the authors noted that raters identified 44% of "Other" criteria not anticipated or defined in the established rubric. The authors explore the challenges and benefits raters perceived in using teaching portfolios as evidence of teaching quality and examine the "other" qualities that raters found significant enough to comment on and use to distinguish the nominee as excellent.

The practice of recognizing excellent teaching through awards in higher education has met with varying degrees of approval in North American universities as well as in the higher education literature. Much of the literature is descriptive in nature, summarizing teaching awards, and providing insight into whether awards provide incentive for good teaching (Chism & Szabo, 1997) or are perceived as popularity contests (Svinicki & Menges, 1996). There is a general concern expressed within the literature that award processes lack clear standards (see, for example, Menges, 1995). This concern is reinforced by the lack of existing research regarding the use and effectiveness of criteria in the selection of teaching award winners.[1] Chism (2005) began to narrow this gap by examining the relationship between the standards used to determine teaching effectiveness and the actual evidence provided. She found that none of the schools studied provided publicly-available standards for judging. Furthermore, her study revealed a large variety of evidence being asked of award nominees and broad categories of judging criteria that lacked explicit standards.

---

1. There do appear to be some differences between faculty and TA awards, but there is very little literature about this. We found only two studies that discuss TA awards specifically (Langford, 1987; Willingham-McLain & Pollack, 2006), which is surprising since there are many universities like Ohio State that use a large number of graduate students as TAs to teach undergraduate courses, and many of these schools have TA awards. This study will add much needed literature and research about this practice.

At The Ohio State University, the Graduate School has been administering the Graduate Associate Teaching Award (GATA) for the past 12 years. In collaboration with the teaching center, the University Center for the Advancement of Teaching (UCAT), efforts have been made to address the aforementioned challenges, such as providing more concrete, transparent criteria as well as to align materials requested from award nominees with those criteria.

In order to be considered for the GATA, graduate student nominees must create and submit teaching portfolios that contain the evidence upon which the nominees are judged according to criteria.[2] Chism (2005) asserts that a very small number of award programs studied used complete and purposefully-defined teaching portfolios as is done in the GATA award process. Because formal studies on the reliability and validity of teaching portfolios are non-existent (Knapper & Wright, 2001), the question of how best to assess teaching portfolios has not been adequately addressed (Centra, 2000). Carusetta (2001) states that the use of portfolios in award processes is best when nominees are provided with (1) a template, (2) the opportunity for consultations with the teaching center, (3) explicit criteria, (4) appropriate amounts of time to develop one, and (5) a selection committee that meets and discusses the judging standards.

This study aims to answer many of the same research questions asked by Chism (2005) and similar ones touched on by Willingham-McLain & Pollack (2006) by investigating one specific award selection season for the GATA. Through this study, we attempt to answer the following research questions.

1. What criteria are selection committee members using to evaluate the portfolios?
2. Is there consistency among selection committee members in the criteria used?
3. How difficult do selection committee members perceive the process of evaluating portfolios as evidence of teaching quality?

This study further addresses a gap that currently exists in the literature about teaching awards: how does a selection committee use criteria to judge teaching effectiveness via teaching portfolios? Answering this question is essential to understanding a practice in which many universities and colleges around the country engage annually. The unprecedented detail of the data collected from this study can inform other institutions' decision-making processes for graduate student teaching awards as well as offer insights that have the potential of being extrapolated for faculty teaching awards.

---

2. This idea was adapted from practice at Duquesne University. They have published a description of their award process (Willingham-McLain & Pollack, 2006).

The Graduate Associate Teaching Award (GATA)

The GATA, awarded since 1973, is the university's highest recognition of exceptional teaching provided by graduate students and has a very high reputation on campus. Ten teaching associates from across the university are given the GATA every spring term and the award is open to all disciplines. Winners receive a $1500 monetary award and plaque. In order to meet the qualifications for the GATA, graduate student nominees must demonstrate excellence in teaching and a commitment to professional development in a teaching portfolio. The nomination portfolio has been adjusted over time to include different items. In 2006, the year in which this study occurred, the portfolio consisted of the following:[3]

- Description of teaching responsibilities (1-2 pages)
- Summary of evaluative feedback (1-2 pages summarizing feedback from students, colleagues, and supervisors)
- Up to three representative student evaluations (or a summative evaluation report from one course)
- Teaching statement (1-2 pages)
- One teaching artifact with explanation and context (1 page)
- Letter of recommendation from a faculty member or administrator (plus an optional letter from one student)

Staff from the teaching center consult with the Graduate School on the requirements for the teaching associate nominees, co-facilitate the training for selection committee members in advance of the adjudication process, and offer workshops and individual consultations with nominees as they prepare their teaching portfolios. Teaching center staff do not rate portfolios during the judging process. Their consulting role with the nominees allows the center to be engaged in the process, yet does not place it in the position of a teaching evaluator; this set of responsibilities is consistent with the center's mission.

Award Selection Committee

The twelve-member selection committee for the GATA was comprised of two undergraduate honors students, two graduate students appointed by Ohio State's Council of Graduate Students, four faculty members who had previously won a University teaching award, and five recent winners of the GATA.

Until 2006, GATA nominees were judged largely on the basis of student evaluation scores, and limited classroom observations (see Chapter 4 of this volume for more details). Because the use of robust nomination portfolios was new in 2006, the Graduate School and the teaching center conducted an hour and a half training session with the selection committee. The goals of the train-

---

3. More details about the award and nomination portfolios are found in Chapter 4 of this volume.

ing were to familiarize members with the nomination portfolio components and to develop criteria for the award process. Training began with a conversation on their general perceptions of what makes a "good" teacher and how one can tell this both in person and in writing. Next, the group discussed the benefits of the nomination portfolio, which included the ability for nominees to provide a context for their teaching goals and strategies—something not easily gleaned through surprise classroom observation visits. The portfolios also afforded the judges (and nominees) the benefit of written reflection on teaching practices and growth.

The majority of the meeting focused on specific portfolio sections and possible criteria. Due to the newness of the portfolio process, no judging criteria were embedded in the initial call for nominations. The call asked nominators (students, faculty, administrators, or the teaching associate themselves) to "describe [their] reasons for nominating the teaching associate and refer to qualities [they] believe make the teacher outstanding" in 150-250 words. It referred them to a list of "qualities that characterize past GATA winners" such as superior organizational and communication skills, excellent and varied teaching techniques, ability to stimulate thinking, and willingness to reflect on feedback. Some of the traits listed were parallel to Ohio State's student evaluation system, which is viewed with skepticism by many. As stewards of the award process, the teaching center and the Graduate School viewed this as an excellent opportunity to create criteria in a constructivist fashion, which not only drew on the collective expertise of the selection committee, but also created for them a high level of ownership and buy-in of the process.

Selection criteria, although finalized with the committee, were initially drafted in consultation with the teaching center and based on existing literature on excellent teaching skills. The criteria were primarily based on Duquesne University's award process and discussions with staff from its teaching center (see Willingham & Pollack, 2006 for their list). Three categories of criteria emerged. The first, Excellent Teaching Indicators, is derived from the basic teaching principles found in Duquesne's version as well as those found in other literature (Bain, 2004; Marincovich, 1997). The second, Positive Student/Teacher Interactions, while also an element of successful teaching, was emphasized because of its significance due to the large size of our institution and the consequent importance placed on creating a more engaged classroom experience for students, the campus culture regarding teaching, and the significant role teaching associates have in courses. The third, Professional Development, has always been a mainstay of the GATA award as a vehicle to help prepare future faculty and was derived from literature on reflecting on teaching (Brookfield, 1995; Willingham-McLain & Pollack, 2006).

Prior to the training, committee members were asked to review and assess three example portfolios at home with the initial list of criteria. The committee then normed their scores, discussed specific examples of the traits, and agreed on where in the portfolio one would find evidence of those traits. There was wide agreement that what was being judged was the teaching quality as evidenced in the portfolio, and not the portfolio itself. By the end of the training, the committee came to an agreement on the criteria list and scoring sheet (Appendix A).

Once all of the nomination portfolios were turned in, each committee member received a subset to rate over the course of several weeks. The members were given the ratings sheet to keep track of their individual scores. Finally, the committee met two times as a group to discuss scores, ask questions, and select 10 winners from the 86 nominees who submitted portfolios that year.

Research Methodology

Twelve subjects participated in this study. All were members of the 2005-06 GATA selection committee who were chosen by the Graduate School in February 2006. To answer the first two research questions regarding criteria and consistency, we collected both their written notes and ratings and observational data. Axiomatic to this research is a belief that, if the committee members wrote something down on their ratings sheets or stated something verbally during the meetings, then that was an important characteristic for them that shaped their evaluation of the portfolios. We observed, audio recorded, and took notes during the two face-to-face meetings of the selection committee. Eleven selection committee members attended each of the meetings. We used a data collection sheet that mimicked the committee members' rating sheet to write down phrases stated by committee members throughout the meetings, and the committee members' comments were placed in the appropriate categories on the sheet. After the meetings, we coded each word or phrase (n=194) according to the corresponding criteria list set in the first meeting.

In addition to the data collected at the face-to-face meetings, we also examined the notes section of the portfolio rating sheets completed by each selection committee member. The committee rated a total of 86 nomination portfolios, with each committee member rating about 35 portfolios. All committee members were asked to use the rating sheets and write notes on the sheets so they would be able to refer to these notes during discussion at the face-to-face meetings. Ten of the 12 selection committee members provided us their rating sheets at the end of the second meeting. We typed all comments on these sheets into a database and coded them by committee member, portfolio number, and section of the rating sheet (listed by the four criteria). A total of 1108 comments were collected and all were included in our original data set. A total of 1057 of those comments were used, as the rest were nonsensical or so non-specific as to be uninterpretable (examples include "No" and "Yes").

To answer the third research question regarding difficulty of the review process, we interviewed volunteer selection committee members. All 12 members were eligible to participate in the interview process. Six agreed to participate and interviews were conducted in July and August 2006 after GATA winners had been announced in June. Each interview lasted between 30 and 45 minutes. See Appendix B for the interview questions. Audio recordings were taken during these interviews and were later transcribed. The interviewer asked 12 open-ended questions of each participant regarding the suitability of the teaching portfolio in the award process and the criteria used by the committee to assess teaching via the portfolios. The interviewer also asked for clarification when necessary. The interviewees consisted of two teaching associates and four faculty; there were five males and one female.[4]

Data Analysis

Initially, the data from the collection sheets (used during the face-to-face meetings and for the notes section of the rating sheets) were coded as corresponding to specific criteria generated by the committee. If a comment did not align with any of the original criteria, it was marked as "other." A secondary content analysis was done on the written comments coded as "other" in order to determine emergent themes. Once themes were identified, comments marked as "other" were coded relative to an additional set of criteria (see Table 1), which were grouped together by the broader categories into which they fell. These same categories were then applied to our content analysis of the verbal comments made during the committee meetings and were used to guide our interpretation of the interview data from which we abstracted themes and patterns arising from how selection committee members perceive the rating process and the use of portfolios as evidence of teaching quality.

A content analysis was done to identify additional emerging themes evident in the language used by committee members both verbally and in writing, as they compared and rated portfolios. Preliminarily we wrote down words and phrasings with no overarching themes or subsets (about 200 codes). We then organized those words and phrases around similar themes and coded all comments. We had two researchers recode all comments and then refined those themes. Final coding was done with an additional new coder on all comments that were left as unknown or un-coded.

Findings

Criteria Used to Evaluate Portfolios

About half of the time the committee members used language that coincided with the initial criteria discussed in the training session and listed on their rating sheets. Out of all of the comments made in the notes they wrote on

---

4. In the Data Analysis and Findings sections, we have identified the participating selection committee members as "raters" for linguistic thrift.

their rating sheets, 56% (n=587) were about either Excellent Teaching Indicators (24%, n=247), Positive Student/Teacher Interactions (11%, n=119), or Professional Development (21%, n=221). However, 44% (n=470) of the time they focused on items not included in their original agreed-upon criteria. To determine why elements beyond those in the original criteria were addressed by committee members, we determined that the 44% of comments could be delineated into three sub-categories: (1) criteria that should have been included in the original list, (2) criteria that are understandably used for differentiating excellent nominees, but not necessarily ones that should have been included in the original list, and (3) traits that are neither appropriate nor intended criteria, but were used to judge teaching. When we applied these three new categories, the comments only fell into the latter two categories. A detailed analysis of those comments is provided below.

(1) Criteria that should have been included in the original list

None of the comments in the 44% met our requirements for this sub-category because the original three categories were broad and inclusive. As we discuss below, there are several traits that for some institutions could merit inclusion on their criteria list.

(2) Criteria that are understandably used for differentiating excellent nominees, but not necessarily ones that should have been included in the original list (37%, n=391)

A large proportion of the comments fall into this sub-category. It makes sense that they appeared in the rating sheet notes and meeting discussions because at some point one needs to find ways to distinguish excellence from greatness. We encourage other institutions to consider the emergence of the following traits as normal and necessary, but not as actual indicators of excellent teaching. We address our reasons below.

Table 1: "Other" categories (44% of the total 1057 coded comments)

Category	% of comments
Rater Objectivity	1%
Length of Teaching Experience	3%
Level of Teaching Responsibility	3%
External Indicators	8%
Quality of Student Evaluations	10%
Portfolio Construction	19%

External Indicators (8%, n=93)

This category included any references to characteristics of the portfolios that were not directly related to the teaching and learning experiences that happened within the confines of a nominee's course—such as whether the nominee had won other awards, the tone of the recommendation letters submitted as part of the portfolio, and how many nominations (and from whom they came) the teaching associate had received as part of the award process. Examples include: "Won department competition to teach course" and "seems like a form letter from recommender."

These same themes emerged during the face-to-face interviews with the committee members, and more than one committee member indicated frustration about this particular category of comments beyond the boundaries of the formal evaluation criteria. As is apparent with these sample comments, some committee members were swayed in opposite directions by the same traits, such as whether they thought student or faculty voices should carry more weight in their deliberations:

"[I looked at] student recommendations—I thought they were more objective than the supervisors or peers." (Rater 4)

"I was incredibly influenced and informed by positive letters based on supervisors or faculty members visiting and observing the class. That's a more direct form of evaluation." (Rater 5)

We view these external indicators as providing an additional layer of evidence about teaching, but these are arbitrary for our teaching associates. Some departments do not have their own internal award, others campaign for their students' nominations, and a few have staff or faculty who regularly observe their teaching associates teach while others do not. We interpret these indicators as commentary on being a very large research university where teaching holds a variable status among different departments and programs rather than a true reflection of a certain nominee's qualifications for a teaching award.

Quality of Student Evaluations (10%, n=101)

Comments in this category had to do with nominees' student evaluations, specifically related to the Student Evaluation of Instruction (SEI) which is Ohio State's standardized, quantitative end-of-term evaluation tool. Comments centered around how they indicated improvement over time or how they compared to their departmental peers. Examples include: "SEIs do not show much improvement" and "High SEIs, especially compared to department."

During the interviews, three of the committee members mentioned that they relied on student evaluations—in some cases heavily:

"I ended up using evaluations as tie-breakers, [especially] within disciplines." (Rater 2)

"I was looking for things I could compare objectively—like SEI scores." (Rater 4)

The GATA specifically rewards a teaching associate's professional development and there is a section in the portfolio to share ways he or she has used this evaluation data to improve and grow as a teacher. Obtaining high scores was not on the original criteria list because this in itself is not what makes someone a good teacher. Since discussion about how to handle and interpret SEIs did not surface in the training, members often used their own judgment about their significance. Additionally, not all teaching associates are eligible to use the SEI (due to their roles or course numbers) and, for those who are, not all departments use the SEI. The tool has a highly politicized status at our university and although getting buy-in from each committee member on how to interpret the SEI scores would have been challenging, we can certainly see how other institutions would view them as integral evidence of one's teaching ability.

Portfolio Construction (19%, n=197)

Finally, the bulk of the comments outside the boundaries of the agreed-upon criteria were about portfolio construction. These included whether the nominee came across as authentic ("Egomaniac—serious questions about the legitimacy of feedback"), choices about what was included in the portfolio ("Would have liked to see a syllabus included"), coherence of the portfolio pieces ("Teaching statement ties closely to other materials"), and general writing skills ("Really good writer").

As with the other categories, the interview comments reflected the themes identified in written comments collected from the committee members' scoring sheets. Several committee members remarked on the elevation of writing ability as a deciding criterion during the rating process, though they generally felt that this was not a particularly relevant or fair way to judge a person's teaching ability.

> "The portfolio is, just by its nature, weighted toward people who are good at writing and I think some very good teachers aren't necessarily good at creative writing." (Rater 6)
>
> "Just because someone could articulate themselves really, really well, I don't think that illustrates or demonstrates to me that they're a great teaching assistant. I mean, it's probably a good thing that they can articulate themselves. I'm a great writer. That doesn't mean I'm a great TA." (Rater 1)

As the last selection committee member implies, and as was presented and agreed upon in the training, the GATA is not an award for writing the best portfolio. However, it becomes clear to readers rather quickly that nominees need to write a coherent narrative about their teaching skills in order to convey their excellence as teachers. In the two nominee information sessions, the teaching center consultant addressed the importance of clear, coherent writing as it was an integral part of discussions about each portfolio component. The teaching center also offered the option of individual consultations to all nominees. In 2006, teaching center staff met with 33 of the nominees, most of whom came in more than once for a total of 56 consults. Teaching center staff focused much of their feedback on organization and coherence of the portfolio, as well as helping nominees make decisions about which examples and details to share in the process of demonstrating their teaching excellence. See Chapter 4 for more details on the GATA nominee experience.

(3) Traits that are not appropriate nor intended criteria, but were used in some cases to judge teaching. (7%, n=79)

Rater Objectivity (1%, n=13)

The few comments in this category included those where raters acknowledged their own subjective preferences for certain nominees such as which department they were from, rather than on the stated "objective" criteria. Though the mere existence of this category points to the difficulty of differentiating between a number of excellent and deserving nominees, fortunately the number of comments was low. This indicates that subjective preference, though present, did not ultimately dominate the decision making process.

Length of Teaching Experience (3%, n=32)

Comments in this category included those that mentioned positively, negatively, or neutrally the amount of time a teaching associate had been teaching. Examples included: "Only taught for one quarter. Too soon to evaluate" and "Extensive teaching experience."

The Graduate School explicitly stated to the selection committee and nominees that the GATA rewards excellent teaching and development by teaching associates, not how long they have been doing it or in what capacity they teach. Our university has a wide range of assistantships and prefers to have one award for all of them. For example, some teaching associates progress to greater degrees of teaching responsibility over time, beginning as a grader and then moving into full responsibility for their own course, while others will be assigned a recitation section for the entirety of their graduate career regardless of their experience or teaching success. Both master's and doctoral students are eligible for the award, so incorporating experience as a criterion inadvertently marginalizes students who are in shorter degree programs. Other institutions may want to consider if this model is appropriate for them, and if so, what role experience and responsibility play in the criteria. It appears natural that committee members would use these traits as criteria in order to differentiate candidates despite directions to not do so. As members state below, the use of a portfolio to share experiences in text consequently highlights these traits.

Level of Teaching Responsibility (3%, n=34)

Committee members were as likely to comment on the length of someone's teaching experience as they were on the perceived difficulty and variety of a teaching associate's teaching experience. This included references to the different levels of responsibility a teaching associate might have (grader, independent instructor, guest lecturer), the types of students a teaching associate might have taught (majors versus non-majors), and other variables such as whether the nominee had previously taught at other universities. Some examples include: "Developed several classes independently" and "Limited experiences and responsibilities."

When the committee members were interviewed, two commented on their shared perception that greater levels of teaching responsibility were more amenable to the portfolio format because teaching associates teaching their own courses had more say over what they did in the classroom.

> "The portfolio, I think, is a little bit easier for students to work with who are coming from disciplines where they are autonomous instructors. [They have] relative advantage… Certain courses that TAs teach are more amenable to what they document." (Rater 3)
>
> "The thing I liked best was the teaching artifact, but again that seems unfair because in some classes they have more leeway." (Rater 4)

Consistency Among Selection Committee Members in the Criteria Used

After we coded the aggregated comments, we looked at each individual rater's comments to ascertain whether any one committee member had disproportionately influenced the overall data. The number of comments from raters ranged from five (<1% of the comments) to 355 (33% of the comments), with a median of 81 comments. A t-test showed that all raters were statistically different (p<.01) from each other in the distribution of their comments. There was no change in significance when we removed the raters with the lowest and highest number of comments. The significant variation between raters indicates that although there was no pattern to their comments, there was also no single rater that skewed the data.

Perceived Difficulty of Evaluating Portfolios as Evidence of Teaching Quality

When asked in the interviews, most committee members stated that the portfolios provided adequate information to judge someone's teaching ability and that they believed the process was fair. Though they generally felt very positive about their experience on the selection committee, they opined that the portfolio favored nominees in certain departments, those with more responsibilities, and those with creative and polished writing ability. One of the biases that came up several times in the interviews was the inherent challenge with the portfolio medium. Not all nominees followed the guidelines or "put equal amounts of effort into it" as Rater 4 stated. He concluded, "in reading over [the portfolios] you felt compelled to support the ones that had a better packet, but I don't know if its just because they had a better packet or they were better TAs."

When asked what they found difficult about the process, raters indicated frustration with the criteria used by their fellow committee members—especially when it came down to ranking the top portfolios. Raters perceived these judgments as biased and not always about criteria on the original list. As Rater 2 depicted, "I have to say, I *kind of* used those rating sheets… I think almost everybody came up with our own ideas about what those things mean." Rater 1 concluded, "I felt like we were all looking at different things." Only Rater 5 commented specifically on the number of criteria. He stated, "I thought there were almost too many evaluation indicators to keep track of, and some were overlapping."

Several raters commented on the influence of perceived personal bias in the competition. Rater 4 suggested that bias was inevitable, explaining, "Sometimes in the packets, in the reflective statements, sometimes the candidates would strike a chord with the rater and that would stick with them throughout the process and they would keep coming back to that, like an emotional connection." Another, Rater 2, stated, "There was someone who let her personal beliefs get involved in how she evaluated things. Like, one, she didn't agree with what someone was teaching, but it seemed to me she was letting her personal biases get involved."

The use of criteria not included on the original criteria list was determined justifiable when it came down to ranking the top portfolios. Rater 3 recalled, "The only time it feels unfair is when you're making the distinction between the top ten and maybe the next two or three. It becomes arbitrary at that point. We're splitting hairs, we're into minutiae, we're sometimes making a decision to diversify by discipline or by college—things that are extraneous to the nominee." For some, the portfolio became less important as the field of possible winners narrowed. Rater 4 stated, "When it came time to narrow it down from 20 to 10, it got harder. The portfolio became less important, because at that point everyone had a good one. So, they were helpful in narrowing it down—to take it from 87 to 20 was pretty good. But realistically, when you look at the top 20, no matter who you pick is going to be a good TA to win the award, so for me it was marginally less important."

During the face-to-face interviews, each of the committee members interviewed mentioned that a way to mitigate some of the challenges with the portfolio would be to add either classroom observations of the nominees' teaching or interviews. For example, Rater 6 explained, "It [the portfolio] doesn't tell the whole picture." Similarly, Rater 2 commented, "I think there should be some type of component that lets us see what the person is like, like an interview or an observation." Adding a component of this sort surely would lend additional depth to the committee's perception of the nominees as teachers. However, several raters recognized that these methods have some of the same potential challenges as the portfolio. Rater 1 commented, "I think both of those [interviews and observations] would be excellent…to have one person from the committee observe, but again you may have some bias there or some inconsistency with what they think is a good teaching technique." Rater 2 added, "I think I like classroom observation. I actually like them both [but] I don't trust how other people on the panel would use the classroom observation."

Conclusions

Both the selection committee and the nominees (see Chapter 4 of this volume) find the process of constructing a teaching portfolio to be an appropriate and valuable part of the GATA process.

As we saw from our in-depth look at one selection committee's experience, identifying excellent teaching is a difficult process. Many variables come into play specifically when using teaching portfolios. We have no reason to assume that our committee's experience would be markedly different than one at another institution; in fact, at our institution, the conversations around the indicators and portfolios are the same year after year, despite the addition of new committee members and continuous refining of the criteria list. There is an obvious need to help the selection committees navigate through the portfolio components, its intended purposes, and potential limitations, as well as create and adhere to agreed-upon standards and practices. As Chism (2005) recommends, teaching center staff can play an important role in these award competitions because they have the expertise to assist in identifying potential evidence, judging standards, and criteria for awards. Positive relationships with the sponsor of the award and defined roles are imperative, especially when a teaching center is involved in a process that is not its own.

The training facilitated for the committee was several hours long and included some initial practice examples. At that time, we thought the norming process was sufficient to adequately prepare the members to adjudicate the portfolios using strictly the criteria we co-created. We have several conclusions based on our experience, one being a reminder that we all instinctually or intuitively define good teaching according to our personal perspectives and can have very strong biases around those definitions. A second is that we do not know what those definitions or biases are unless we make them visible. Using additional criteria (e.g., level of teaching responsibility, evaluation scores) to determine winners in a pool of several excellent and deserving teachers may ultimately be necessary. Therefore, one should plan for open discussion wherein these additional criteria can be addressed. One effective strategy is to use sample portfolios beforehand to explicitly surface these preferences from the beginning, rather than letting them bubble up at a point where there is little time to address them or it is too late to change committee members' minds.

In 2006 we decided to create our initial criteria list based on indicators for excellent teaching that were supported by the literature. What we did not anticipate was the inclination of the committee members to use other evidence such as letters of recommendations and previous awards for teaching. Although it is understandable that these were used for differentiating excellent nominees (as discussed above), these are not appropriate as criteria for our award because of the specific institutional context and culture. Committee members clearly disagreed on this matter despite the effort put forth to norm their approaches to scoring portfolios. Therefore, having clear guidelines on the use of these criteria upfront and allowing for discussion amongst the committee about how to distinguish among exceptional teachers is imperative.

One of the initial reservations about using teaching portfolios for the GATA was that writing quality would unjustly dominate the decision making process, despite the fact that the purpose of the award was to identify *excellent teaching* rather than an *excellently written portfolio*. However, because a teaching portfolio is a written document meant to represent a non-written experience, the skill with which the nominee is able to communicate in writing what they do in the classroom will likely always bear on the judging process in some measure. This is not necessarily a problem—especially if one considers that using teaching portfolios in the awards process provides graduate students with opportunities to work on their communication skills in a broader context than their home discipline. With the significant number of comments about writing quality made during the 2006 GATA selection process, our belief in its importance seems warranted. From this we conclude that teaching centers must provide numerous opportunities for award nominees to better articulate their teaching stories as they develop as instructors and construct portfolios.

When we explicitly asked our interviewees about other sources of evidence beyond the portfolio, they clearly wanted to do classroom observations, interviews, or both. For some institutions, these options may be plausible. However, there are some limitations that may make a face-to-face component impractical, such as a lack of available time on the part of the committee, situations in which nominees are not teaching during the term the award decisions are being made, and, as with the teaching portfolios, variability in the interpretation of the criteria for evaluating a nominees teaching via observation or interview. In fact, these limitations were what initially contributed to our institution's decision to convert from an observation to a teaching portfolio system for the award.

We suspect that if observations or interviews were included in award adjudication, committees would have similar concerns and challenges as ours did with the portfolios, and those would likely align with the comments we found. If an institution decides to implement teaching observations or student interviews as part of the process, one option would be to use teaching portfolios to narrow down the nominees to a list of semifinalists who would be observed before the committee made their final selections. In fact, there is a graduate teaching associate award issued by one of the colleges within Ohio State that uses this model. Teaching portfolios could be used to inform the observations or interviews, as they would provide meaningful context on a teacher's goals, process, reflectiveness, and development, which one could not obtain otherwise. Without this context and discussion about excellent teaching criteria, there is a risk of committee members focusing predominantly on presentation skills, as was the case in previous years at our institution.

Based on our findings, we suggest others institute a facilitated norming process that involves bringing committee members together to work with sample portfolios, observation reports, or interview notes, and to ask questions to ensure (as much as possible) shared interpretations of the stated criteria for judging. The award process should be regularly assessed and criteria refined to most effectively reflect and direct the conversations of future selection committees. This case study provided us with valuable information on the benefits and realities of using portfolios in a teaching associate award. We hope other institutions can use the data to inform their own practices.

Future Directions

We have been involved in the GATA selection process for many years and we have found the data from 2006 to be anomalous to other years. However, an obvious limitation of this study is that the data were derived from one institution, in this one year, with only one selection committee. There is a need for more people to study their own processes and not just take for granted that it all works out for the best. Although we assume we can probably generalize to other institutions (particularly research-extensive universities), the literature could benefit from studies about other teaching awards and specifically about processes that include observations and/or interviews with nominees.

References

Bain, K. (2004). *What the best college teachers do.* Cambridge, MA: Harvard University Press.

Brookfield, S. D. (1995). *Becoming a critically reflective teacher.* San Francisco, CA: Jossey-Bass.

Carusetta, E. (2001). Evaluating teaching through teaching awards. In C. Knapper & P. Cranton (Eds.), *New Directions in Teaching and Learning: No. 88. Fresh approaches to the evaluation of teaching* (pp. 31–40). San Francisco, CA: Jossey-Bass.

Centra, J. A. (2000). Evaluating the teaching portfolio: A role for colleagues. In K. E. Ryan (Ed.), *New Directions in Teaching and Learning: No. 83. Evaluating teaching in higher education: A vision for the future* (pp. 87–93). San Francisco, CA: Jossey-Bass.

Chism, N. V. N. (2005). Promoting a sound process for teaching awards programs: Appropriate work for faculty development centers. In S. Chadwick-Blossey & D.R. Robertson (Eds.), *To Improve the Academy: Vol. 23. Resources for faculty, instructional, and organizational development* (pp. 314–330). Bolton, MA: Anker.

Chism, N. V. N., & Szabo, B. L. (1997). Teaching awards: The problem of assessing their impact. In D. DeZure & M. Kaplan (Eds.), *To Improve the Academy: Vol. 16. Resources for faculty, instructional, and organizational development* (pp. 181–200). Stillwater, OK: New Forums Press.

Knapper, C., & Wright, W. A. (2001). Using portfolios to document good teaching: Premises, purposes, practices. In C. Knapper & P. Cranton (Eds.), *New Directions in Teaching and Learning: No. 88. Fresh approaches to the evaluation of teaching* (pp. 19–29). San Francisco, CA: Jossey-Bass.

Langford, T. A. (1987). Recognizing outstanding teaching. In N. V. N. Chism (Ed.), *Institutional responsibilities and responses in employment and education of teaching assistants: Readings from a national conference* (pp. 132–133). The Ohio State University: Center for Teaching Excellence.

Marincovich, M. (1997). Training new consultants at Stanford: The TA consultants program. In K. Brinko & R. Menges (Eds.), *Practically Speaking: A sourcebook for instructional consultants in higher education (*pp. 305–326.). Stillwater, OK: New Forums Press.

Menges, R. J. (1995). Awards to individuals. In M. D. Svinicki & R. J. Menges (Eds.), *New Directions in Teaching and Learning: No. 65. Honoring exemplary teaching* (pp. 3–9). San Francisco, CA: Jossey-Bass.

Svinicki, M. D., & Menges, R. J. (1995). Consistency within diversity: Guidelines for programs to honor exemplary teaching. In In M. D. Svinicki & R. J. Menges (Eds.), *New Directions in Teaching and Learning: No. 65. Honoring exemplary teaching* (pp. 109–113). San Francisco, CA: Jossey-Bass.

Willingham-McLain, L., & Pollack, D. (2006). Exploring the application of best practices to TA awards: One university's approach. In S. Chadwick-Blossey & D.R. Robertson (Eds.), *To Improve the Academy: Vol. 24. Resources for faculty, instructional, and organizational development* (pp. 247–258). Bolton, MA: Anker.

Stephanie V. Rohdieck is the Associate Director of the University Center for the Advancement of Teaching at The Ohio State University. She teaches courses on college teaching and teaching support for graduate teaching assistants. Her current research interests are graduate teaching preparation, teaching portfolio development, diversity, teaching awards, clinical teaching, and instructional consultation.

Dawn Walts is an Assistant Professor of English at Lewis University. She specializes in Medieval Literature, Shakespeare, and First-Year Writing. She was a recipient of the Graduate Associate Teaching Award at The Ohio State University in 2005.

Lindsay Bernhagen is an Instructional Consultant in the University Center for the Advancement of Teaching at The Ohio State University. She earned her PhD in Comparative Studies at Ohio State. She was a recipient of the 2012 Graduate Associate Teaching Award.

Kathleen M. Hallihan is the Director of Admissions and Student Services for the John Glenn School of Public Affairs at The Ohio State University. She teaches courses on college teaching and specializes in academic strategic planning, program assessment and accreditation at all levels. She is an accreditor with the Western Association of Schools and Colleges, and is the advisor for co-curricular programs such as the Ohio Student Education Policy Institute. She directed the Preparing Future Faculty Program at Ohio State from 2004-2007.

Appendix A
Graduate Associate Teaching Award Selection Criteria

The Graduate Teaching Associate being nominated demonstrates....

Criteria	Evidence	Location/ examples
A. Excellent Teaching Indicators	Prepares for teaching (course is well-thought out and lessons are prepared in advance)	
	Is organized (course and class)	
	Is clear in explanations about content	
	Uses teaching methods appropriate for learning goals	
	Designs materials for class that are purposeful	
	Materials meet goals set in course	
	Materials are creative, can take original materials and make them better	
	Can explain how materials meet learning objectives	
	Is flexible - can accommodate spontaneous discussion about content	
	Evaluates student learning in appropriate and varied ways (exams, labs, papers, etc.)	
	Assessments (exams, labs, etc.) allow students to demonstrate their knowledge of the subject	
B. Positive Student-Teacher Interactions	Can build a positive student-teacher rapport with most students	
	Is available to students in and out of the classroom	
	Is ethical (fairness in grading, appropriate interactions with students, etc.)	
	Is culturally sensitive (understands student diversity issues, creates an inclusive classroom)	
	Prompt in returning feedback to students	
	Encourages enthusiasm (for learning, in general and content)	
	Encourages students' engagement in learning, the class, and the content	
	Attentive to student learning needs and can assist with problem-solving when necessary	
	Encourages informal communication with students in order to be able to "read" class for potential issues	
	Has good listening skills	
	Can communicate on a student level (is aware of audience when teaching)	

Continued on next page.

C. Professional Development as a Teacher	Has well-defined goals for themselves as a teacher	
	Has enthusiasm about teaching	
	Initiates formal feedback mechanisms at end of quarter	
	Asks for mid-quarter feedback (from students, peers, advisors, consultants, etc.)	
	Reflects on student feedback	
	Makes changes to teaching based on feedback	
	Articulates professional development (progress) as a teacher	
	Explains why he/she teaches the way that he/she does	
	Seeks out professional development opportunities/ interactions	
D. What about this candidate, if anything, makes him or her stand out from all of the other outstanding nominees?		

Appendix B
Selection Committee Member Interview Questions

1. What did you like about being on the selection committee?
2. What did you dislike about being on the selection committee?
3. Is a portfolio an appropriate way to get evidence on teaching excellence? Why or why not?
4. Would you have preferred to gather data about a TAs teaching ability in another way? If so, how? (Examples: classroom observation, interviews, etc)
5. Do you believe you were able to make fair decisions, in general, about the quality of a TA's teaching ability?
6. Now that you have used the criteria for many nomination portfolios, were there specific things that you felt you concentrated on more than others? Anything not on the list that you used?
7. Was it difficult to differentiate between excellent TAs? Why or why not? What about it made it difficult? How could that have been made easier for you, if at all?
8. Do you think the portfolio provides a positive developmental process for graduate students (regardless of whether or not they win)? Why or why not?
9. Do you think being on the selection committee helped you in your own development as a teacher? If so, how?

Chapter 8
A Model of Professional Development for Graduate Student Teaching

A. Ahmad & J. M. Barrington[1]

This article describes a model of professional development for graduate student teaching. Participants build a teaching dossier that can help them in their careers as teachers. We argue that a solid foundation for professional development is necessary for graduate teaching to be assessed, recognized, and rewarded in any meaningful way.

Graduate Student Teaching in Canada

Despite the proliferation of teaching awards offered by Canadian institutions, which mirrors the growth of similar awards elsewhere in the world, graduate teaching awards at any level (institutional, regional or national) are scarce. Several reasons might explain this including the very orientation of graduate programs that are geared to teach content, research methodologies, and other applied skills. Furthermore, as Simmons (2007) reports, the great majority of courses on teaching that do exist are not associated with a program or curriculum and are almost never a pre-requisite for a teaching appointment. Although similar in content and objectives (Schönwetter, Ellis, Taylor, & Koop, 2008), according to Knapper (2012), none of these graduate teaching courses are assessed in any robust or meaningful way.

Institutions, therefore, continue to face a double challenge of (1) creating interventions for graduate students that ensure they obtain a set of relevant teaching skills, and (2) recognizing evidence of outstanding graduate teaching.

We propose to frame this double challenge through the lens of professional development. Our argument is based on the assumption that teaching skills and good educational practices must be systematically provided to graduate students as a foundation before their teaching and leadership potential can be assessed, recognized, and rewarded in any meaningful way.

---

1. We wish to acknowledge the contributions of graduate students: Justin Ible for collecting and analyzing evaluation data related to the graduate seminar in university teaching described in this article and Stephanie Hobbis for her invaluable comments and editing.

In other words, we acknowledge the importance of paying closer attention to the role of graduate teaching awards, as demonstrated in this special edition of *Studies in Graduate and Professional Student Development*, yet we contest that these awards are only viable when implemented in a context that favors graduate students' professional development at large.

On Teaching Awards

Research remains skeptical about the value of teaching awards in general. Chism and Szabo (1997) argue that while teaching awards affirm recipients' confidence they hardly ever inspire others. Frame, Johnson, and Rosie (2006), themselves winners of the UK's National Teaching Fellowship, find little correlation between teaching awards and an improved value of teaching in comparison to research; and because processes for recipient selection are not always methodologically sound and transparent, suspicion about their validity persists (Badri & Abdulla, 2004; Chism, 2006). On the other hand, teaching awards are generally regarded more favorably if they are part of a larger professional development ecology. Berk (2005) argues that "The merits of teaching awards should be evaluated in the context of an institution's network of incentives and rewards for teaching" (p. 55); and Weimer (1991) suggests, "Teaching awards work successfully when they represent one of many ways in which instructional excellence and efforts to achieve it are recognized, valued, and rewarded" (p. 136).

Therefore, we want to use this space to describe a model of professional development for graduate student teaching that we are confident can be replicated in any higher educational setting. We also suggest criteria for rewarding graduate student teachers that is more than recognizing that they are naturally good at teaching. We go beyond graduate teaching to describe criteria for leadership potential proposed by the Canadian Society for Teaching and Learning in Higher Education (STLHE). We hope that, over time, this foundation will serve graduate students to build a teaching dossier that can be systematically evaluated for teaching awards and help them in their careers as teachers.

A Model of Professional Development for Graduate Student Teaching

Central to the success of Concordia University's academic plan is a coherent and comprehensive program of graduate student training in teaching. A multi-pronged approach has been created based on a developmental model of professional development: from minimum training for all teaching assistants, to training for tutorial leaders, to training for graduate students assigned reserve courses (Reilly, 2012). The model comprises six professional development interventions that are continuously evolving.

Orientation for Teaching Assistants

Traditionally, the orientation for teaching assistants (TA) has been a full agenda of administrators talking about roles and responsibilities and faculty and staff facilitating sessions on active learning, or critical incidents around grading, for example. We have experimented with disciplinary-specific orientations to better meet the needs of students in Engineering and Computer Science or Arts and Sciences. On average, 200 graduate students have attended, mostly from Engineering because they require attendance for a TA contract. This rate of attendance is less than 10% of the number of unique TA contracts across the university. To dramatically raise attendance we are experimenting with two new interventions. One is an online training program that covers basic teaching skills (described below) and the other is a World Café design for the face-to-face orientation.

The World Café is a participatory dialogue method for engaging people in conversations that matter (http://www.theworldcafe.com). A graduate student with experience in this method has been hired and we are involving TAs in the design and execution of the event. Our objectives include: (1) fostering a culture of dialogue and conversation; (2) creating a space for TAs to unpack their questions, concerns, and reflections about their role; (3) facilitating networking among TAs to help create a sense of belonging within the larger university and a community of support; (4) introducing TAs to the resources available to them; (5) introducing TAs to our new online modules as a valuable support reference for their role in the classroom. We anticipate that the new design will result in a greater number of TAs attending the orientation and engaging in further teaching-related professional development.

Online Modules on Basic Teaching Skills

In anticipation of mandatory TA training that would involve three hours of training for about 1,500 (mostly) graduate students each year, we are also experimenting with online learning. We have purchased an existing program developed by Epigeum (www.epigeum.com), a spin-off company from Imperial College London, and endorsed by Graham Gibbs and Diane Laurillard. Several North American universities are using the program with positive results. For example, Michigan State University uses the program for TA training (1,200 students) and for faculty development. They use it in their workshops for discussion purposes and in their Certificate in Teaching program (150 students) by assigning the online modules as homework. We are using it in similar ways.

The program is designed in a series of modules, of which we are pilot-testing four: Marking, Grading and Giving Feedback; Making the Most out of

Discussion; Lecturing Skills; and Principles of Course Design. Each module takes about 120 minutes to complete. The modules have been uploaded into Moodle (Concordia's course management system) and customized to our needs (rearranged, retitled, and pages added and deleted). We have also included our own content on plagiarism and Concordia's Academic Code.

These new and exciting opportunities for graduate students have yet to be tested. The reason for mentioning them here is to reinforce our main argument that teaching awards have to be integrated into a larger context of professional development to be effective. Our signature offering described next has been the focus of rigorous evaluation and research.

Graduate Seminar in University Teaching (GSUT)

Concordia's Centre for Teaching and Learning Services (CTLS) has been offering a Graduate Seminar in University Teaching (GSUT) for the past nine years. The seminar is part of the Centre's mandate rather than an academic department in order to make it accessible across the disciplines. Initially, a 25-hour non-credit seminar was designed in a 10-week format and offered free of charge to doctoral and terminal master's students. In 2010, significant funding was leveraged so that the seminar could be opened to all masters students. An intensive one-week format was added in the spring and summer semesters. Since its inception, over 800 students have successfully completed the seminar.

CTLS staff and a multi-disciplinary team of faculty and graduate students teach the seminar and a TA is assigned to each section. A senior lecturer in Computer Science receives a course remission to teach a section specifically for Engineering and Computer Science students. A Fine Arts section has also been added taught by the Visual Resources Coordinator who is also a part-time faculty member. A section specifically for science students was offered in the fall of 2011 taught by a Lecturer in Psychology. We also experimented with a multi-disciplinary section co-taught by two facilitators from different disciplines (Applied Human Sciences and Education).

The overall goal of the GSUT is for students to examine current issues relating to teaching and learning in higher education, and to develop competence in making instructional decisions appropriate to their subject domain. Inspired by Saroyan and Amundsen's (2004) course design and teaching workshop, the seminar provides students with an opportunity to discuss their views on teaching and possibly change their conceptions from a content orientation (focusing on what should be covered) to a learning-orientation (focusing on how to teach so that students learn well). A summary of the main topics and theories taught is included in Appendix A.

A series of activity-based lesson plans has been developed, as well as PowerPoint slides, handouts, and a Moodle website. There is a nominal charge of $10 for handouts and students purchase a required text: On Course: A week-by-week guide to your first semester (Lang, 2008). The estimated time commitment for students is 25 hours in-class and 10 hours out-of-class for preparation of readings and assignments. Students receive a certificate of participation for engaging in class discussions and complete the following requirements: write a teaching philosophy statement, plan a lesson and teach a 10 minute excerpt, and prepare a concept map and syllabus for a course they would like to teach. These learning outcomes enable students to produce artifacts they can use when applying for a teaching position.

Evaluation data on the GSUT was systematically collected over a three-year period. On the question "How useful was this seminar to your work/academic experience", on a scale of 1-4 (with 4 being extremely useful) the weighted average was 3.52 in 2010 (n=209); 3.39 in 2011 (n=160); and 3.51 in 2012 (n=113). These results are similar across all sections regardless of format (weekly or intensive), instructor (faculty teaching award winners and lecturers vs. educational development staff and graduate students), and whether it is a discipline-specific or multi-disciplinary section. In written comments, students say they enjoy the mini-lesson component the most and their recommendation for the future is to have a longer duration. They want the chance to practice, get feedback, and practice again, especially for the mini-lesson. In other words, there is something in the GSUT experience itself that is useful for students and can lead to deep and meaningful learning.

Assessing whether learning has actually taken place is more challenging than eliciting feedback. In 2010, a graduate student in Education investigated the GSUT as part of his master's thesis (Ible, 2011). Using a paper-based questionnaire (see Appendix B), students rated themselves on the last day of the seminar in relation to a set of 10 learning outcomes on a scale from 1-5 (with 5 being very high) both prior to the seminar (n=205) and immediately after the seminar (n=204). Alumni of the seminar were asked the same questions in a follow-up survey three months later (n=70). The largest gain in cumulative means was in the students' ability to articulate their own teaching philosophy statement (2.08 prior, 3.91 immediately after, and 3.77 three months later). The teaching philosophy statement is repeatedly given as a major benefit of the seminar due to its importance for teaching applications. The second largest gain was in their ability to articulate attainable learning outcomes (2.16 prior, 4.05 immediately after, and 3.98 three months later). The third was in their ability to design a course syllabus based on a concept map of the content (2.02 prior, 4.05 immediately after, and 3.82 three months later). This positive change from before to after the seminar is to be expected following any well-designed instructional intervention. What is unexpected is that when answering the same question three months later students perceived an enduring sense of achievement.

Deeper investigation into the GSUT is the focus of a program of research funded by a Canadian Social Sciences and Humanities Research Council

(SSHRC) Insight Development Grant titled, *Examining Interdisciplinary Perspectives to Educate Tomorrow's Teachers in Canadian Higher Education.* The broad research questions include: (1) assessing outcomes of graduate students learning to teach; (2) identifying disciplinary-specific examples and ways of thinking in the context of generic pedagogical approaches; and (3) examining student artifacts, focus group discussions and instructional practices to reveal differences in generic and disciplinary approaches to teaching. The GSUT research team meets once a month and has hired three GSUT alumni graduate students and one undergraduate student as co-collaborators.

To get a sense of the scope of inquiry some team members, in subgroups, have already (a) devised a coding scheme that discerns the quality of teaching philosophies to corroborate with quantitative analyses; (b) designed the parameters of a qualitative analysis and coding of concept maps using the chain, spoke and network designations, as proposed by Hay, Kinchin, and Lygo-Baker (2008); and (c) conducted a confirmatory and exploratory factor analysis of GSUT students using the Phenomenographic Pedagogy and Revised Approaches to Teaching Inventory (Trigwell, Prosser, & Ginns, 2005). Furthermore, we have obtained ethics approval from participants to analyze more systematically three GSUT assignments: the teaching philosophy statement, concept map, and course outline. We plan to triangulate data from these. Some of this work has already been presented at regional conferences and we now look forward to sharing our findings at international conferences.

Student-led Community of Practice

As mentioned, many students have expressed a desire to continue to meet after the GSUT ends prompting the idea of creating a community of practice (CoP) to complement and extend the experience. This initiative was proposed by two graduate students, one of whom has been involved in the GSUT for many years as a TA and is now teaching her own section and working as a research assistant. As described in their proposal, the aim of the CoP is "to provide a space where graduate students, after having successfully completed the GSUT, can participate in continued conversations about their teaching experiences while engaging in activities that would further promote the development of knowledge and practice of effective and dynamic teaching" (Blom & Esseghaier, 2012, p.1). A modest grant has been provided for experimentation and over twenty students have eagerly signed up for the experience. This is the first volunteer project actively promoted by the CTLS and we look forward with interest to the outcome.

Follow-up Pedagogical Workshops

Since it was first established over forty years ago, the CTLS (previously called the Learning Development Office) has provided pedagogical workshops for faculty and welcomed attendance by graduate students. Recently the university has taken considerable interest in the professional development of graduate students. Our School for Graduate Studies now offers workshops in a range of skill domains including teaching and knowledge transfer (see their website for details: http://graduatestudies.concordia.ca/gradproskills/). These pedagogical workshops are provisioned by the CTLS and this year's topics include: Planning Your First Day of Class, Social Media, Appreciative Pedagogy, Flipping Your Classroom, and Experiential Learning. These short workshops have become very popular since they are easy for students to fit into their schedule and do not require any additional commitment in terms of readings and assignments.

New Graduate Certificate in University Teaching

The latest addition to our institution's model of professional development is a new Graduate Certificate in University Teaching offered by the School of Graduate Studies. It is a 15-credit program restricted initially to doctoral candidates to give them a competitive edge when applying for tenure-track positions. The GSUT is a prerequisite for admission as well as the identification of a teaching mentor in the student's department, and a letter of support from the department chair guaranteeing that a course will be reserved for a teaching internship. Course work includes an existing Education course on Learning Theories, a Seminar on Teaching and Learning in Higher Education, and a unit on the Development of a University Course. The capstone requirement is to teach a 3-credit university course in the student's area of specialization.

This new initiative not only institutionalizes the GSUT but also adds credence to our own research efforts. It is within this kind of context that criteria for graduate student teaching awards are best established because awards that are not integrated into a wider framework remain questionable in their achievements and wider validity. The GSUT and other interventions not only play an important role in advancing graduate students' involvement in the teaching community and knowledge of good practices, but also equip students with the skills that are necessary to be recognized and rewarded for excellence in teaching.

Criteria for Graduate Student Teaching Awards

According to Chism (2006) and Gibbs (2007) there are no clear-cut criteria to judge excellence for teaching awards. In some cases "excellence is not [even] defined by the scheme... what 'good' or 'excellent' teaching consists of is considered either self-explanatory, beyond explication or irrelevant" (Gibbs, 2007, p.2). However, in other contexts (and, fortunately, increasingly in most) a set of criteria are provided to applicants that follow, sometimes more and sometimes less, findings of the Scholarship of Teaching and Learning (SoTL) on good teaching practices. Accordingly, a student-centered approach to teaching is one of the most frequent criteria (Chism, 2006) as well as evidence of rigorous reflection about teaching through use of pedagogic literature, personal experiences, and anecdotes (Gibbs, 2007).

Several GSUT components are directly relevant for teaching award applications. Many require teaching philosophy statements. Not only are these a crucial component of the seminar but GSUT instructors also find that participants' teaching philosophies often outdo those of experienced teachers. Less common but existent are requests to include syllabi (20% of the teaching awards surveyed by Chism (2006)). The preparation of syllabi that follow good teaching practices is also a core component of the seminar.

More broadly, the GSUT equips students with general knowledge about how to prepare teaching dossiers (portfolios). While seemingly banal, and a necessary skill set for any instructor at the university level, Carusetta's (2001) analysis of the Stuart Award for Excellence of Teaching demonstrates particular inadequacies. In 1999 only 24 out of 65 nominations included all necessary application documents, and when asked to submit a complete teaching portfolio none of the short-listed candidates had one easily at hand.

This demonstrates not only one of the primary issues with teaching awards, but it also re-emphasizes the importance of programs such as the GSUT which have demonstrated an increase in knowledge about, and positive engagement with, teaching in higher education. They are crucial for elevating the perceived value of graduate student teaching, and indispensible if teaching awards are to become competitive and more closely aligned with excellence in teaching.

Leadership in Higher Education

In the future, we plan to introduce the idea in the GSUT of including an educational leadership statement in the teaching dossier. The element of leadership is what distinguishes the Canadian 3M National Teaching Fellowships Award that honours 10 faculty each year. There is an expectation for nominees to articulate a rationale for going beyond personal teaching practice and to provide evidence of a scholarly approach to teaching and to share best practices and research results with as broad an audience as possible. In other words, besides providing evidence for outstanding teaching practices, the nominee must write a statement of leadership and back up the statement with leadership activities that have extended their impact beyond their discipline and institution.

A similar National Student Fellowships Award recognizes 10 students who demonstrate qualities of outstanding leadership during their undergraduate experience. Examples of leadership include: (a) making a difference to governance or student life; (b) being involved in a significant event within academia or beyond; (c) helping to resolve important issues in higher education; and (d) volunteering, mentoring, or engaging in community-based service learning. Already, this award has had an impact on the Canadian national society for teaching and learning (STLHE). Award-winners design and are featured in a plenary session at the annual national conference. Both these awards are described in detail on the website of the STLHE: www.stlhe.ca.

In conclusion, we hope other professional development efforts in Canada and overseas will adopt a version of what we have found to be very successful. Our main contribution has been aimed to improve the assessment of graduate teaching programs that not only help to decide whether they have an impact, but also to encourage our colleagues to consider what are deemed acceptable standards of graduate teaching programs. Using data from the GSUT, we have demonstrated the impact on student learning and look forward to disseminating results as they continue to emerge from our collaboration.

While our efforts are geared towards improving teacher education of graduate students, we also hope to encourage collaborative efforts with our colleagues to enhance recognition of good teaching practices for both students and teachers and consequently improve students' learning experiences within post-secondary settings.

References

Badri, M.A., & Abdulla, M.H. (2004). Awards of excellence in institutions of higher education: An AHP approach. *International Journal of Educational Management, 18*(4/5), 224–242.

Baxter Magolda, M. (1992). *Knowing and reasoning in college: Gender related patterns in students' intellectual development.* San Francisco: Jossey-Bass.

Berk, R.A. (2005). Survey of 12 strategies to measure teaching effectiveness. *International Journal of Teaching and Learning in Higher Education, 17*(1), 48–62.

Biggs, J.B., & Tang, C. (2007). *Teaching for quality learning at university.* Berkshire: Open University Press.

Bloom, B. S. (Ed.). (1956). *Taxonomy of educational objectives: Handbook I-Cognitive domain.* New York: David McKay.

Blom, M., & Esseghaier, M. (2012). *GSUT Learning Community Initiative - Proposal.* Internal document. Concordia University, Centre for Teaching and Learning Services, Montreal, Canada.

Bucus, D., & Thorbek, R. (Directors). (2006). *Teaching teaching & understanding understanding.* Retrieved from http://www.youtube.com/watch?v=iMZA80XpP6Y&feature=related.

Canadian Association for Graduate Studies (CAGS) in conjunction with The Social Sciences and Humanities Research Council of Canada (October 2012). *Graduate student professional development: A survey with recommendations.* Retrieved from: http://www.cags.ca/cags-publications.html

Canadian Association for Graduate Studies (CAGS) (2008, November). *Professional skills development for graduate students.* Retrieved from: http://www.cags.ca/cags-publications.html

Carusetta, E. (2001). Evaluating teaching through teaching awards. *New Directions for Teaching and Learning, 88,* 31–40.

Chapnick, A. (2004). Training teaching assistants helps everyone. *University Affairs, 45*(3), 40.

Chism, N.V.N. (2006). Teaching awards: What do they award? *The Journal of Higher Education, 77*(4), 589–617.

Chism, N.V.N., & Szabo, B. (1997). Teaching awards: The problem of assessing their impact. In D. DeZure (Ed.), *To improve the academy: Yearbook of the Professional and Organizational Development Network in Higher Education* (pp.181–199). Stillwater, OK: New Forums Press.

Csikszentmihalyi, M. (1991). *Flow: The psychology of optimal experience.* New York: Harper & Row.

Frame, P., Johnson, M., & Rosie, A. (2006). Reward or award? Reflections on the initial experiences of winners of a National Teaching Fellowship. *Innovations in Education and Teaching International, 43*(4), 409–419.

Gagne, R. M., Briggs, L. J., & Wager, W. F. (1985). *Principles of instructional design,* Belmont, CA: Wadsworth.

Gibbs, G. (2007). Judging teaching excellence for teaching awards: Theory, policy and practice. *Higher Education Academy Conference.* Retrieved from http://ebookbrowse.com/gibbs-2007-judging-teaching-excellence-for-teaching-awards-theory-policy-and-practice-doc-d20065004

Hay, D., Kinchin, I., & Lygo-Baker, S. (2008). Making learning visible: the role of concept mapping in higher education. *Studies in Higher Education, 33*(3), 295–311.

Ible, J. (2011). *University alignment of graduate student instructor development: A maximal variation exploration.* (Unpublished master's thesis). Concordia University, Montreal, Canada.

Kirkpatrick, D.L., & Kirkpatrick, J.D. (2006). *Evaluating training programs: The four levels* (3rd ed.). San Francisco: Berrett-Koehler.

Knapper, C. (2012). The impact of training on teacher effectiveness: Canadian practices and policies. In Simon, E. & Pleschov, G. (Eds.), *Improving teaching in higher education: The challenges of creating effective instructional development programs.* London: Routledge.

Knorr, K., McCurdy, T., & Vajoczki, S. (2010). *Developing development: A systematic methodology for a formalized faculty development program.* Hamilton, Ontario; McMaster University Centre for Leadership in Learning.

Kolb, D.A. (1984). *Experiential learning: Experience as the source of learning and development.* Englewood Cliffs, NJ: Prentice Hall.

Krathwohl, D. (2002). A revision of bloom's taxonomy: An overview. *Theory into Practice, 41*(4), 212–218.

Mezirow, J. (1991). *Transformative dimensions of adult learning.* San Francisco: Jossey-Bass.

Perry, W. G. (1970). *Forms of intellectual and ethical development in the college years: A scheme.* Troy, MO: Holt, Rinehart & Winston.

Reilly, R. (2012). *Teaching assistant training initiative proposal.* Internal document. Concordia University, Centre for Teaching and Learning Services, Montreal, Canada.

Saroyan, A., & Amundsen, C. (Eds.) (2004). *Rethinking teaching in higher education: From a course design workshop to a faculty development framework.* Sterling, VA: Stylus.

Schön, D. A. (1983). *The reflective practitioner: How professionals think in action.* San Francisco: Jossey-Bass.

Schönwetter, D. J., Ellis, D. E., Taylor, K. L., & Koop, V. (2008). An exploration of the landscape of graduate courses on college and university teaching in Canada and the USA. *Studies in Graduate and Professional Student Development, 11*(1), 7–29.

Simmons, N. (2007). *What's different under the gown: New professors' development as university teachers.* Unpublished doctoral thesis, Brock University, St. Catherines, Ontario.

Soloman, B., & Felder, R. (n.d.). *Index of learning styles questionnaire.* Retrieved from http://www.engr.ncsu.edu/learningstyles/ilsweb.html

Trigwell, K., Prosser, M., & Ginns, P. (2005). Phenomenographic pedagogy and a revised Approaches to teaching inventory. *Higher Education Research & Development, 24*(4), 349–360.

Weimer, M. E. (1991). *Improving college teaching.* San Francisco: Jossey-Bass.

A. Ahmad is Associate Professor in the John Molson School of Business at Concordia University in Canada; President of the Society for Teaching and Learning in Higher Education; and Vice-President of the International Consortium for Educational Development consisting of 23 member organizations worldwide. His academic career has focused on pedagogical innovation, collaborative inquiry and professional development. In 1992, he was recognized for leadership in teaching with a lifetime 3M National Teaching Fellowship – a program he coordinated for 10 years.

J. M. Barrington is a Teaching Consultant at the Centre for Teaching and Learning Services, Concordia University, Canada, where she has worked for the past 12 years. She teaches a Graduate Seminar in University Teaching and is engaged in a Social Sciences and Humanities Research Council funded project on the seminar studying the teaching support needs and challenges of current and prospective teachers. Her current interest is in the interdisciplinary scholarship of teaching and learning.

Appendix A
Overview of Seminar Topics

1. Teaching Philosophy Statement (TPS). In class, students share memories of their favorite teachers and the characteristics they embody. A set of metaphor cards drawn specifically for the seminar helps them to reflect upon their unique approach to teaching. Students engage in a simulated meeting of a departmental personnel committee to select an interviewee based on four sample statements. A list of "do's" and "don'ts" in writing a TPS is generated from this exercise. Students submit a draft, and receive extensive feedback for improving their TPS.

2. How students learn. Students are introduced to four theoretical frameworks. They complete either Felder's learning styles inventory (Solomon & Felder, NA) or an abbreviated version of Kolb (1984). They play the "Perry Game" which requires categorizing a set of statements that students would typically say into the intellectual development theory of William Perry (1970) and Baxter Magolda (1992). They discuss a video on student approaches to deep vs. surface learning (Bucus & Thorbek, 2006) and are introduced to the constructive alignment theory of John Biggs (2007). They also reflect on the importance of motivation in learning and Csikszentmihalyi's (1991) theory of "Flow."

3. Course design. Students are guided through a principled approach to instructional design based on concept mapping showing how course elements relate to each other and how philosophy statements guide these. Several maps are presented and handed in for feedback. Students are introduced to Bloom's Revised Taxonomy of Learning (Bloom 1956; Krathwohl, 2002) and encouraged to write higher order learning outcomes that encourage deep approaches to learning.

4. Assessment of learning. This topic is often discussed and demonstrated in several sessions and focuses on the use of rubrics for developing grading criteria and formative techniques for checking understanding and repairing misconceptions. Students select appropriate assessment methods for the course they have designed so that these are aligned with their stated learning outcomes.

5. Lesson Planning. Students are introduced to a lesson plan template that emphasizes clear presentation of content and the active engagement of students among other elements. In preparation for their individual mini lessons, a number of teaching strategies and techniques are highlighted as well as a set of effective presentation skills.

6. Uses of technology. This session often involves clickers and demonstrations from guest lecturers of online courses and colleagues who have made effective interventions using innovative technologies. The CTLS has produced screencasts of guest lectures on social media, learning objects, blogging, etc. for students to view online.

7 & 8. Mini-lessons. Students teach a 10-minute lesson to put principles into practice. They give feedback on each other's work and provide some of the most memorable moments of the seminar.

9. Ethical and classroom management issues. Students are quick to provide great examples, incidents, and dilemmas that evoke intense discussion, debate and assessment of institutional policies designed to guide teaching and student behaviours.

10. The teaching dossier and simulated interviews. By the last class students have generated personal examples and artifacts that they can document as part of their craft in their teaching dossiers. Mock interviews based on actual questions used in CEGEPs help to prepare students for the job market.

Appendix B
Questionnaire

**Graduate Seminar in University Teaching
Participant Evaluation**

Instructor and date:

Please take a few minutes to complete this questionnaire. Your participation will help us improve future programming. Your responses are anonymous. We will not ask for your name. Thank you for your cooperation.

1. Select one from each column that best describes you: [Degree level; Discipline]

2. How useful was this seminar to your work/academic interests? [1. Not at all; 2. Somewhat; 3. Very; 4. Extremely]

3. What did you like the most about this seminar?

4. What are your most important suggestions to improve this seminar?

5. What is your most significant take away from this seminar?

	6. The GSUT aims to help you to achieve the outcomes listed below. Please let us know how you would rate yourself on each item below prior to this seminar, and now, at the conclusion of this seminar. Remember that this evaluation is anonymous.	Prior to Seminar					Now				
		1=Very Low	2=Low	3=Moderate	4=High	5=Very High	1=Very Low	2=Low	3=Moderate	4=High	5=Very High
a.	Your ability to articulate your own teaching philosophy statement.	O	O	O	O	O	O	O	O	O	O
b.	Your knowledge of good practices in university teaching.	O	O	O	O	O	O	O	O	O	O
c.	Your knowledge regarding how students learn.	O	O	O	O	O	O	O	O	O	O
d.	Your knowledge of different teaching strategies.	O	O	O	O	O	O	O	O	O	O
e.	Your ability to design a high quality lesson.	O	O	O	O	O	O	O	O	O	O
f.	Your confidence to deliver a lesson that captures the attention of students.	O	O	O	O	O	O	O	O	O	O
g.	Your ability to design a course syllabus based on a concept map of the content.	O	O	O	O	O	O	O	O	O	O
h.	Your ability to articulate a set of attainable learning outcomes.	O	O	O	O	O	O	O	O	O	O
i.	Your ability to design appropriate assignments.	O	O	O	O	O	O	O	O	O	O
j.	Your ability to adopt a student-centered approach to teaching.	O	O	O	O	O	O	O	O	O	O
k.	Your confidence in making instructional decisions appropriate to your subject domain.	O	O	O	O	O	O	O	O	O	O
l.	Your confidence in using technology to promote student learning.	O	O	O	O	O	O	O	O	O	O
m.	Your preparedness to apply for a teaching position.	O	O	O	O	O	O	O	O	O	O

7. Please feel free to share any other comments you might have. Thank you very much.

www.ingramcontent.com/pod-product-compliance
Lightning Source LLC
Chambersburg PA
CBHW072151160426
43197CB00012B/2337